R Bruce

Columbia May '64

50th Anniversary Edition

The Federal Reserve System

1913 ★ 1963

THE
Federal Reserve System

PURPOSES AND FUNCTIONS

BOARD OF GOVERNORS

of the Federal Reserve System

Washington, D. C., 1963

First Edition – May 1939
Second Edition – November 1947
Third Edition – April 1954
Fourth Edition – February 1961
Fifth Edition – December 1963

Library of Congress Catalog Card Number 39-26719

FOREWORD

THIS fifth edition of *The Federal Reserve System: Purposes and Functions* commemorates the fiftieth anniversary of the signing of the Federal Reserve Act by President Woodrow Wilson on December 23, 1913. As with earlier editions, the book is dedicated to a better public understanding of the System's trusteeship for the nation's credit and monetary machinery.

To this end, this new edition has been expanded to include chapters on the organization of the Federal Reserve System for policy-making, on the open market policy process, and on the balance of payments. These and other changes that have been made throughout the text are designed to clarify the System's role and functioning in light of changes that have occurred in the national and world economies and in light of further advances in monetary knowledge. Improvement in content and organization has been undertaken with the single objective of making the subject matter more understandable to the reader.

This edition, like former ones, is a collaborative product of the Board's staff. Ralph A. Young, Adviser to the Board, was responsible for coordinating and supervising the staff work that went into its preparation.

BOARD OF GOVERNORS
OF THE FEDERAL RESERVE SYSTEM

Washington, D. C.
December 1963

ACKNOWLEDGMENTS

THE content and arrangement of this anniversary edition has benefited from suggestions by many readers and critics of previous editions, by members of the Board's staff, and by other readers in the Federal Reserve System. All of these suggestions are here acknowledged with appreciation.

The preparation of the present edition, with its considerable reorganization and expansion, has been carried out with the close collaboration of Stephen H. Axilrod, Senior Economist, Division of Research and Statistics. He assumed responsibility for planning and development of the content and had immediate charge of integrating revised text.

The new chapter on the balance of payments was prepared by A. B. Hersey, Adviser, Division of International Finance, and the chapter on the open market policy process by Peter M. Keir, Senior Economist, Division of Research and Statistics. Other members of the Board's staff who contributed to the improvement of various chapters were: Frederic Solomon, Director, Division of Bank Examinations; J. Herbert Furth, Adviser, Division of International Finance; and Lewis N. Dembitz and Robert Solomon, Associate Advisers, Division of Research and Statistics. In addition, special acknowledgment is made to Guy E. Noyes, Director, Division of Research and Statistics, for his criticisms of substance during the revision of the book.

ACKNOWLEDGMENTS

Valuable suggestions in their special areas were received from Robert C. Masters, Associate Director, Division of Bank Examinations; M. B. Daniels, Assistant Director, Division of Bank Operations; Charles A. Yager, Chief of the Government Finance Section, Division of Research and Statistics; Normand R.V. Bernard, Economist, Division of Research and Statistics; and Henry N. Goldstein and Margaret R. Garber, Economists, Division of International Finance.

For editorial work in preparing the text for publication, special credit is due to Elizabeth B. Sette, Chief of the Economic Editing Unit, Division of Research and Statistics. Helen R. Grunwell supervised the illustrations, and Jean King prepared the index.

The previous edition of the book benefited greatly from the interest and suggestions of Woodlief Thomas, formerly Adviser to the Board, and of Susan S. Burr, formerly Associate Adviser, Division of Research and Statistics. Many of their contributions to the preceding edition carry over into this one.

RALPH A. YOUNG

CONTENTS

CHAPTER   PAGE

I. FUNCTION OF THE FEDERAL RESERVE SYSTEM.... 1

An efficient monetary mechanism is indispensable to the steady development of the nation's resources and a rising standard of living. The function of the Federal Reserve System is to foster a flow of credit and money that will facilitate orderly economic growth, a stable dollar, and long-run balance in our international payments.

II. STRUCTURE OF THE FEDERAL RESERVE SYSTEM... 15

Administration of monetary policy and other Federal Reserve functions is carried out through the Federal Reserve System, which includes twelve Federal Reserve Banks, the Board of Governors in Washington, and the Federal Open Market Committee. All national banks and many State banks are members of the System. This organization is especially adapted to a banking system with many independent banks.

III. INSTRUMENTS OF MONETARY REGULATION...... 29

The principal means by which monetary policy achieves its objectives are open market purchases and sales, mainly of U. S. Government securities but also of foreign currencies; discount operations; and changes in reserve requirements. Regulation of stock market credit supplements these means of influence. Use of all the instruments is closely coordinated.

CONTENTS

CHAPTER   PAGE

IV.   FUNCTION OF BANK RESERVES..................   63

      Bank reserves constitute both the legally required
      basis and the functional basis of bank deposits.
      Changes in the reserve position of banks, therefore,
      directly affect the flow of bank credit and money.
      In carrying out its central responsibility, the Fed-
      eral Reserve System relies primarily on its ability
      to increase or decrease the volume and cost of bank
      reserves.

V.   THE CREDIT MARKET.......................   83

      Commercial banks are part of the national credit
      market, which is made up of many interrelated
      markets. Developments in all parts of the market
      interact on other parts. Neither the banking sector
      nor the nonbanking sectors of the market can be
      understood by themselves.

VI.   INTEREST RATES............................   107

      Interest rates are the prices paid for borrowed
      money. They are established in credit markets as
      supplies of and demands for loanable funds seek
      balance. Movements of interest rates are influenced
      by the nation's saving and investment, by market
      expectations, and by the flow of bank credit and
      money.

VII. INFLUENCE OF RESERVE BANKING ON ECONOMIC
      STABILITY................................   127

      Federal Reserve influence on the flow of bank credit
      and money affects decisions to lend, spend, and save
      throughout the economy. Reserve banking policy
      thus contributes to stable economic progress.

CHAPTER   PAGE

VIII. THE BALANCE OF PAYMENTS.................... 149

Our economy is part of the world economy. Prices and interest rates here interact with prices and interest rates abroad, and the interrelationships affect our international balance of payments. In its decisions on monetary policy the Federal Reserve has to take the U. S. balance of payments into account. Operations by the System in foreign exchange markets help to cushion unusual supply or demand pressures in these markets.

IX. RELATION OF RESERVE BANKING TO GOLD...... 165

Gold flows, which generally reflect balance of payments conditions, are an important influence on member bank reserves. Inflows of gold reduce the reliance of banks on Federal Reserve credit, and outflows of gold increase it. Changes in the country's monetary gold stock are reflected in Federal Reserve Bank holdings of gold certificates.

X. RELATION OF RESERVE BANKING TO CURRENCY... 177

The Federal Reserve System is responsible for providing an elastic supply of currency. In this function it pays out currency in response to the public's demand and absorbs redundant currency.

XI. BALANCE SHEET OF THE FEDERAL RESERVE BANKS. 187

Federal Reserve functions are reflected in the consolidated balance sheet of the Reserve Banks, known as the weekly condition statement. This statement shows how much Federal Reserve credit is being used and the key items that account for its use.

CONTENTS

CHAPTER   PAGE

XII.   THE BANK RESERVE EQUATION............... 199

Federal Reserve credit, gold, and currency in circulation are the principal factors that influence the
volume of member bank reserves—the basis of bank
credit and the money supply. The relationship among
these factors, together with other more technical
ones, is sometimes called the bank reserve equation.

XIII.   SHORT-TERM CHANGES IN BANK RESERVES...... 215

Reserve banking policy responds to all of the elements that affect member bank reserve positions. A
full accounting of bank reserve factors is published
each week in a table accompanying the Reserve Bank
condition statement.

XIV.   ORGANIZATION FOR MONETARY POLICY......... 225

The Board of Governors has a central role in achieving coordinated use of all of the instruments of
monetary policy, and it maintains close relations with
other policy-making agencies in the Government.
Federal Reserve Banks play an important part in
System policy through representation on the Federal
Open Market Committee and through their responsibilities for discount operations.

XV.   THE OPEN MARKET POLICY PROCESS........... 235

In deciding on reserve banking policy, account must
be taken of all the economic forces at work in the
domestic economy as well as of those affecting relations with the rest of the world. Complexities of the
economic situation require that reserve banking
instruments be used flexibly, with the nature of the

banking process making for central reliance on
open market operations. As a result, the formulation
of open market policy and the conduct of operations
in the market are at the heart of the policy process.

XVI.   SUPERVISORY FUNCTIONS OF THE FEDERAL RESERVE   257

By keeping individual banks strong and by maintaining competition among banks, bank supervision
helps to maintain an adequate and responsive banking system. This contributes to the effective functioning of monetary policy and of economic processes generally.

XVII.   SERVICE FUNCTIONS......................   267

The Federal Reserve Banks handle the legal reserve
accounts of member banks, furnish currency for
circulation, facilitate the collection and clearance of
checks, and act as fiscal agents of the U.S. Government.

SELECTED FEDERAL RESERVE PUBLICATIONS.....   279

INDEX...................................   287

ILLUSTRATIONS

PAGE

Money and Near-Moneys............................ 7

Map of the Federal Reserve System................. 16

The Federal Reserve System: Organization........... 22

Government Security Transactions, 1962............. 36

Discount and Bill Rates........................... 48

Federal Reserve Credit........................... 59

Process of Deposit Expansion...................... 72

Deposits and Bank Lending........................ 76

Member Bank Reserves........................... 79

Credit Expansion................................. 84

Rates on Bank Loans to Business................... 86

U. S. Government Marketable Debt................. 89

Change in Financial Position...................... 93

Gross National Saving............................ 94

Coupon Rate, Market Yield, and Price.............. 109

Long- and Short-Term Interest Rates............... 111

Selected Interest Rates........................... 113

Yields and Prices on U. S. Government Securities..... 115

Flow of Federal Reserve Influence.................. 129

Gross National Product and Money Supply.......... 146

U. S. Balance of Payments........................ 153

ILLUSTRATIONS

PAGE

Total U. S. Gold Stock.............................. 168

Reserves of Federal Reserve Banks................... 173

Kinds of Currency.................................. 179

Currency in Circulation............................. 181

Currency and Federal Reserve Credit................. 183

Disposition of Federal Reserve Bank Earnings......... 196

Bank Reserve Equation.............................. 203

Production and Prices............................... 209

Reserves and Borrowings............................ 222

The Federal Reserve System: Relation to Instruments of
    Credit Policy.................................... 227

Relationships among Reserve Measures............... 250

Checks Handled by Reserve Banks................... 272

The Federal Reserve System

The Federal Reserve System

CHAPTER I

FUNCTION OF THE FEDERAL RESERVE SYSTEM. *An efficient monetary mechanism is indispensable to the steady development of the nation's resources and a rising standard of living. The function of the Federal Reserve System is to foster a flow of credit and money that will facilitate orderly economic growth, a stable dollar, and long-run balance in our international payments.*

O N December 23, 1913, President Woodrow Wilson signed the Federal Reserve Act establishing the Federal Reserve System. Its original purposes, as expressed by its founders, were to give the country an elastic currency, to provide facilities for discounting commercial paper, and to improve the supervision of banking.

From the outset, there was recognition that these original purposes were in fact parts of broader objectives, namely, to help counteract inflationary and deflationary movements, and to share in creating conditions favorable to a sustained, high level of employment, a stable dollar, growth of the country, and a rising level of consumption.

1

Acceptance of the broader objectives has widened over the years.

Over the years, too, the public has come to recognize that these domestic objectives are related to the country's ability to keep its flow of payments with foreign countries in reasonable balance over time. Today it is generally understood that the primary purpose of the System is to foster growth at high levels of employment, with a stable dollar in the domestic economy and with over-all balance in our international payments.

How is the Federal Reserve System related to production, employment, the standard of living, and our international payments position? The answer is that the Federal Reserve, through its influence on credit and money, affects indirectly every phase of American enterprise and commerce and every person in the United States. The purpose of this book is to describe the ways in which the Federal Reserve System exerts this influence.

Background of the Federal Reserve System

Before establishment of the Federal Reserve System, the supply of bank credit and money was inelastic. This resulted in an irregular flow of credit and money and contributed to unstable economic development.

Commercial banks in smaller cities and rural regions maintained balances with commercial banks in larger cities, which they were permitted to count as reserves against the deposit accounts of their customers. Large amounts of these reserve balances were maintained in New York and Chicago. Many banks, furthermore, as a matter of convenience and custom and as a means of utilizing idle funds, kept in the financial centers any deposit balances over and above their required reserves. In New York, Chicago, and St. Louis, designated as central reserve cities, national banks were required to maintain all their legal reserves in the form of cash in their own vaults.

Under these circumstances, when banks throughout the country were pressed for funds by their depositors and borrowers, these demands ultimately converged on a few commercial banks situated in the financial centers. In ordinary times the pressures were not excessive, for while some out-of-town banks would be drawing down their balances, others would be building theirs up. But in periods when business was unusually active and the public needed larger amounts of currency for hand-to-hand circulation, the demand on city banks for funds would become widespread and intense. Because of the relatively large role played by agricultural production in that period, credit demand each year was particularly strong during the crop-moving season. At such times banks all over the country would call on banks in the financial centers to supply funds.

Since no facilities were available to provide additional funds, including currency, the credit situation would become very tight. To meet the out-of-town demand for funds, the banks in the financial centers would sell securities and call loans or would refuse to renew existing loans or make new ones. As a result, security prices would fall, loans would have to be liquidated, borrowing from banks as well as other lenders would become difficult, and interest rates would rise sharply. Every few years difficulties of this kind would lead to a sharp liquidation of bank credit. These liquidations were called money crises.

The problem had been under public discussion and study

for a long time when, following a crisis of unusual severity in 1907, Congress appointed the National Monetary Commission to determine what should be done. After several years of thorough consideration, Congress adopted legislation embodying the results of study by the Commission and by other authorities. This legislation was the Federal Reserve Act, which became law on December 23, 1913. The establishment of the Federal Reserve System — which comprises twelve regional Reserve Banks, coordinated by a Board of Governors in Washington — provided machinery by which varying demands for credit and money by the public could be met.

All of the principal nations have institutions, commonly called central banks, to perform functions corresponding to those of the Federal Reserve System. In England it is the Bank of England, which has been in existence since the end of the seventeenth century; in France it is the Bank of France, established by Napoleon I; in Canada it is the Bank of Canada, which began operations in 1935.

The principal function of the Federal Reserve is to regulate the flow of bank credit and money. Essential to the performance of this main function is the supplemental one of collecting and interpreting information bearing on economic and credit conditions. A further function is to examine and supervise State banks that are members of the System, obtain reports of condition from them, and cooperate with other supervisory authorities in the development and administration of policies conducive to a system of strong individual banks.

Other important functions include the provision of cash-balance and payment services to the member banks of the Federal Reserve System, the U.S. Government, and

4

the public. These services are chiefly the following: handling member bank reserve accounts; furnishing currency for circulation and making currency shipments; facilitating the clearance and collection of checks; effecting telegraphic transfers of funds; and acting as fiscal agents, custodians, and depositaries for the Treasury and other Government agencies.

Since the main concern of the Federal Reserve is the flow of credit and money, these words must be given meaning at the outset. This can best be done by considering these four questions: (1) What is money and how is it used? (2) How is money related to other assets with somewhat similar characteristics? (3) By what means does the Federal Reserve regulate credit and money? (4) How do changes in credit and monetary conditions affect people's lives?

Money and Its Uses

Money is most meaningfully defined in terms of how it is used. Money serves as: (1) a means of payment; (2) a standard of value; and (3) a store of purchasing power.

As a means of payment, money allows individuals to concentrate their productive efforts on those activities for which they are best equipped and in which they are trained to engage. Money is what people receive in return for their services and what they use to buy the goods and other things they need for themselves and their families.

As a standard of value, money provides the means by which a day's work can be equated with, for example, a family's food, housing, and other bills, including what is set aside for old age or for children's education. It is thus the measuring rod in terms of which producer and consumer choices can be assessed and decided.

5

As a store of purchasing power, money enables us to set aside some of our present income for future spending or investing. It is a way in which remuneration for labor and work in the present can be stored for meeting the many contingencies, needs, or opportunities that individuals and families are likely to face in the future.

The wide variety of uses for money make it vital and necessary to the functioning of our economic system. If money were impaired as a means of payment, or a standard of value, or a store of purchasing power, the economy's ability to grow and to produce and distribute goods in accordance with the needs and wishes of the people would be jeopardized.

Money and Near-Moneys

In the United States circulating paper money and coins of all kinds (currency) and the demand deposits held by commercial banks perform all the functions of money. When a person has $10 of paper money and coin in his pocket and $100 in his checking account in the bank, he is in a position to spend $110 at any time. These two sums represent his active cash balance; they serve the same general purpose, and each can be converted into the other at any time; that is, currency can be converted into a demand deposit by taking it to a bank, and a demand deposit can be converted into currency by taking it out of a bank.

The amounts of currency and of demand deposits at the end of 1962 are shown in the chart. It will be seen that the amount of demand deposits in commercial banks is far greater than the amount of currency in circulation.

Commercial banks also hold savings and other time

6

deposits, on which an interest return is paid. These deposits are one of the so-called near-moneys shown in the chart.

Savings and time deposits at banks differ importantly from demand deposits. They are not transferable by check.

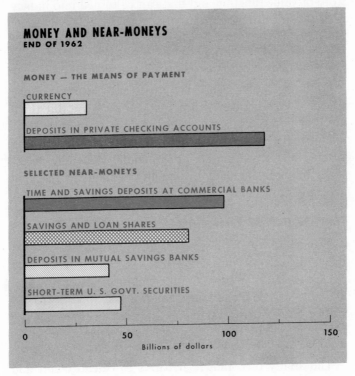

MONEY AND NEAR-MONEYS
END OF 1962

MONEY — THE MEANS OF PAYMENT

CURRENCY

DEPOSITS IN PRIVATE CHECKING ACCOUNTS

SELECTED NEAR-MONEYS

TIME AND SAVINGS DEPOSITS AT COMMERCIAL BANKS

SAVINGS AND LOAN SHARES

DEPOSITS IN MUTUAL SAVINGS BANKS

SHORT-TERM U. S. GOVT. SECURITIES

0   50   100   150

Billions of dollars

While convertible into demand deposits or currency, savings deposits of individuals are subject to prior notice of conversion. In practice, however, they may generally be withdrawn on request. Other time deposits are not payable before maturity except in emergencies. Thus savings and time deposits, while serving a store-of-value function, are

7

not in themselves means of payment; only currency and demand deposits serve in this active monetary role.

In addition to time and savings deposits in commercial banks, there are other interest-bearing assets that serve a store-of-value function and that can be turned into money with little inconvenience and little or no risk of loss in value. Such assets include deposits in mutual savings banks, shares in savings and loan associations, short-term U.S. Government securities, and U.S. Government savings bonds.

For many years now, individuals and businesses have shown a growing preference for near-moneys. But there are limits on the extent to which people can reduce their money balances in favor of other assets. The growing volume of transactions in an expanding economy necessarily requires the ready availability of funds in checking accounts or of hand-to-hand currency.

How the Federal Reserve Influences Credit and Money

Practically all of the money that people use reaches them, directly or indirectly, through banks. They may receive their pay in cash, but the employer who pays them will have cashed a check at a bank or may have borrowed from a bank before making up his payroll. Therefore, the flow of money in the country depends greatly on the ability of commercial banks to make loans and investments.

The ability of commercial banks to extend credit and provide cash-balance and payment services to the people depends on the amount of reserve funds the banks have. This amount is directly affected by Federal Reserve operations. Banks can extend credit to customers or invest money in securities only in proportion to the reserves at their disposal. The way the system of reserves works, and

8

the fact that under it the banks can lend in the aggregate several times as much as they have in reserves, is discussed in Chapter IV.

What needs to be understood first is that the Federal Reserve, by influencing the availability and cost of additional bank reserves, can influence the amount of credit that banks may extend to the public through loans and investments. The reserve position of banks affects directly the willingness of banks to extend credit and the cost, or rate of interest, that borrowers from banks have to pay to obtain it.

As banks extend credit by exchanging bank deposits for the various assets they acquire — promissory notes of businesses and consumers, mortgages on real estate, and Government and other securities — they create demand deposits. These deposits can in turn be used to make payments by check or can be withdrawn for use in the form of currency. Ultimately, they may find their way into banks' time and savings deposits if the public prefers to save in that form. In any event, by affecting the volume of reserves available to member banks, the Federal Reserve has the power to influence the country's over-all credit situation and its money supply.

While the Federal Reserve directly influences the availability and cost of bank credit and thereby affects the total flow of credit, a great variety of other forces also affect the flow of credit in the economy. These include, among others, governmental policies in regard to expenditures, taxes, and debt; the distribution of income among different groups of the population and the allocation of income between current consumption and saving; the bargaining strength and policies of management, labor, agriculture,

9

and other sectors of the economy; the course of foreign trade and foreign investment; the prospects for peace or war; and the expectations of businesses and consumers as to future economic changes, especially price changes.

Thus, the Federal Reserve alone cannot assure favorable economic conditions. Nor can it direct whether bank credit, or any other type of credit, shall flow into particular channels. But it can affect the general flow of bank credit and money as economic conditions change and thus help to counteract instability resulting from other forces. The crucial question for the Federal Reserve is how much expansion in bank credit and money it should encourage in view of current and prospective developments in the domestic economy and in our balance of payments.

How Changes in Credit and Money Affect People

Superficially, it might seem that the more credit and money people have the better off they are. In fact, however, it is not the number of dollars that all the people have available that is important, but what those dollars will buy today as compared with earlier periods and as compared with the future.

People have different tests of whether they as individuals have enough money. To the manufacturer, the test is whether he has or can borrow at a reasonable cost enough dollars to buy his raw materials, pay the wages of his employees, and make other payments necessary to a profitable operation and to a sustained strong credit position. The farmer and the merchant have similar tests.

To the consumer, the test is whether he has or can borrow enough money, at a cost and on repayment terms that he can meet, to buy what he needs. Essentially, people are

10

concerned mainly with what they can do with the dollars they earn, are indebted for, or need to borrow.

The ultimate test, in other words, is the purchasing power of the dollar over time in terms of goods and services. In this respect the usefulness of money is enhanced if the dollar's value, as indicated by the average price level for goods and services, remains reasonably stable.

In a dynamic and growing economy, enough credit and money is that amount which will help to maintain high and steadily rising levels of production, employment, incomes, and consumption and to foster a stable value for the dollar. When credit, including bank credit, becomes excessively hard to get and costs too much, factories and stores may curtail operations and lay off employees. Smaller payrolls mean hardship for workers, who curtail their purchases; merchants feel the decline in trade and reduce their orders for goods. Manufacturers in turn find it necessary to lay off more workers. A serious depression, unemployment, and distress may follow.

When credit is excessively abundant and cheap, the reverse of these developments — an inflationary boom — may develop. An increase in the volume and flow of money resulting from an increase in the supply and availability of credit, coupled with a lowering of its cost, cannot in itself add to the country's output. If consumers have or can borrow so much money that they try to buy more goods than can be produced by plants running at capacity, this spending only bids up prices and makes the same amount of goods cost more. If merchants and others try to increase their stocks so as to profit by the rise in prices, they bid up prices further. Manufacturers may try to expand their plants in order to produce more. If so, they

11

bid up interest rates, wages, and prices of materials. In the end they raise their own costs.

The nation as a whole does not profit from conditions of price inflation. These conditions are typified by closely linked advances in material costs; in wages of workers in industry, trade, and services; in prices of finished products; and in the cost of living generally. In such a situation, the many individuals whose incomes are relatively inflexible suffer a decline in living standards. At some point the upward spiral will break, perhaps because prices of finished goods get so high that ultimate consumers, even though many of them receive higher wages, can no longer buy the goods produced. Then a downward spiral will develop. The more values have risen because of inflation, the more abruptly and lower they are likely to fall and the greater will be the associated unemployment and distress.

Efforts to attain domestic prosperity and price stability go hand in hand with efforts to attain balance in international payments. If this country obtains less funds from its exports of goods and services or from long-term capital inflows than it spends or invests abroad, then we add to our short-term debt to foreign countries and we lose gold from our national monetary reserves. The persistence of such a situation can lead to general loss of confidence in the dollar internationally, to an accelerated outflow of funds from this country, and to a more rapid drain on the nation's gold stock. Thus expansion in bank credit and money has to be evaluated in terms of both its impact on domestic economic growth and its effect on the balance of international payments.

Here, two points that concern the relationship of the balance of payments to domestic economic activity may be noted briefly. First, in the long run an expansion in bank credit and money consistent with reasonable domestic price stability will contribute to balance in our international payments by helping keep goods produced here competitive with foreign products. Secondly, in the short run it is necessary to take account of the influence that domestic credit conditions and costs have on international capital flows, because movements of capital among countries in response to differences in the availability and cost of credit can have disruptive effects on international payments flows and domestic financial markets.

The above recital is oversimplified in that it does not include all the factors that affect the level of economic activity or the flow of payments to other countries. Nevertheless, it does show how the economy is affected if, on the one hand, credit is too scarce or hard to get and too dear or if, on the other hand, it is too plentiful or easily obtainable and too cheap. By influencing the flow of bank credit, with resulting effects on the flow of money and the flow of credit generally, the Federal Reserve System influences the economic decisions that people make, which are reflected in the level of economic activity, in price developments, and in the balance of international payments.

CHAPTER II

STRUCTURE OF THE FEDERAL RESERVE SYSTEM. *Administration of monetary policy and other Federal Reserve functions is carried out through the Federal Reserve System, which includes twelve Federal Reserve Banks, the Board of Governors in Washington, and the Federal Open Market Committee. All national banks and many State banks are members of the System. This organization is especially adapted to a banking system with many independent banks.*

THE Federal Reserve System is designed to combine public and private participation and to serve the public welfare efficiently. Federal Reserve functions are carried out through twelve Reserve Banks and their twenty-four branches and through central coordination by the Board of Governors in Washington. A diversity of experience and knowledge is brought together through this broadly based and unique banking mechanism. This chapter will explain the structure and membership of the Federal Reserve System, while a later chapter will describe how the System is organized for policy-making purposes.

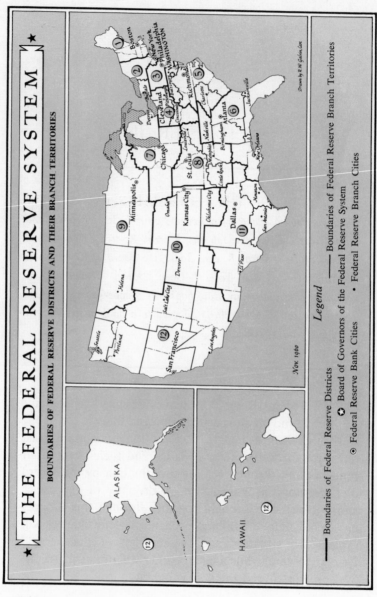

★ THE FEDERAL RESERVE SYSTEM ★

BOUNDARIES OF FEDERAL RESERVE DISTRICTS AND THEIR BRANCH TERRITORIES

Drawn by R.W. Gaston Cast

Nov. 1960

Legend

—— Boundaries of Federal Reserve Districts   —— Boundaries of Federal Reserve Branch Territories

✪ Board of Governors of the Federal Reserve System

◉ Federal Reserve Bank Cities   • Federal Reserve Branch Cities

Federal Reserve Banks

In order that the Federal Reserve might serve the large area and the diverse resources of the United States effectively, the Federal Reserve Act provided that the System be divided into twelve districts. These are shown in the map on the opposite page. The boundaries of the Federal Reserve districts do not always follow State lines, and in many instances part of a State is in one district and part in another.

In each district there is a Federal Reserve Bank, and most of the Reserve Banks have branches. A list of the districts and branches is given below:

Federal Reserve Bank of Boston   District Number 1

Federal Reserve Bank of New York   District Number 2
    Branch at Buffalo, New York

Federal Reserve Bank of Philadelphia   District Number 3

Federal Reserve Bank of Cleveland   District Number 4
    Branches: Cincinnati, Ohio
              Pittsburgh, Pennsylvania

Federal Reserve Bank of Richmond   District Number 5
    Branches: Baltimore, Maryland
              Charlotte, North Carolina

Federal Reserve Bank of Atlanta   District Number 6
    Branches: Birmingham, Alabama
              Jacksonville, Florida
              Nashville, Tennessee
              New Orleans, Louisiana

Federal Reserve Bank of Chicago   District Number 7
    Branch at Detroit, Michigan

17

Federal Reserve Bank of St. Louis   District Number 8
    Branches: Little Rock, Arkansas
               Louisville, Kentucky
               Memphis, Tennessee

Federal Reserve Bank of Minneapolis   District Number 9
    Branch at Helena, Montana

Federal Reserve Bank of Kansas City [1]   District Number 10
    Branches: Denver, Colorado
               Oklahoma City, Oklahoma
               Omaha, Nebraska

Federal Reserve Bank of Dallas   District Number 11
    Branches: El Paso, Texas
               Houston, Texas
               San Antonio, Texas

Federal Reserve Bank of San Francisco [2] District Number 12
    Branches: Los Angeles, California
               Portland, Oregon
               Salt Lake City, Utah
               Seattle, Washington [2]

Decentralization is an important characteristic of the Federal Reserve System. Each Reserve Bank and each branch office is a regional and local institution as well as part of a nationwide system, and its transactions are with regional and local banks and businesses. It gives effective representation to the views and interests of its particular region and at the same time helps to administer nationwide banking and credit policies.

Each of the twelve Federal Reserve Banks is a corporation organized and operated for public service. The Federal

---

[1] Kansas City, Missouri.
[2] Alaska is part of the Seattle Branch territory and Hawaii part of the head office territory of the District.

Reserve Banks differ from privately managed banks in that profits are not the object of their operations and in that their shareholders—the member banks of the Federal Reserve System—do not have the proprietorship rights, powers, and privileges that customarily belong to stockholders of privately managed corporations.

The provisions of law circumscribing the selection of Reserve Bank directors and the management of the Reserve Banks indicate the public nature of these Banks. Each Federal Reserve Bank has nine directors. Three of them are known as Class A directors, three as Class B directors, and three as Class C directors. The Class A and Class B directors are elected by member banks, one director of each class being elected by small banks, one of each class by banks of medium size, and one of each class by large banks.

The three Class A directors may be bankers. The three Class B directors must be actively engaged in the district in commerce, agriculture, or some other industrial pursuit and must not be officers, directors, or employees of any bank. The three Class C directors are designated by the Board of Governors of the Federal Reserve System. They must not be officers, directors, employees, or stockholders of any bank. One of them is designated by the Board of Governors as chairman of the Reserve Bank's board of directors and one as deputy chairman. The chairman, by statute, is designated Federal Reserve Agent and has special responsibilities on behalf of the Board of Governors in Washington.[3]

Under these arrangements, businessmen and others who

---

[3] The Federal Reserve Agent, subject to approval by the Board of Governors, appoints such assistant Federal Reserve agents as he may need in the performance of his duties, which are noted in Chapter X.

are not bankers constitute a majority of the directors of each Federal Reserve Bank. The directors are responsible for the conduct of the affairs of the Reserve Bank in the public interest, subject to supervision of the Board of Governors. They appoint the Reserve Bank officers, but the law requires that their choice of president and first vice president, whose terms are for five years, be approved by the Board of Governors.

Each branch of a Federal Reserve Bank also has its own board of directors. A majority are selected by the Reserve Bank; the remainder, by the Board of Governors.

Board of Governors

The Board of Governors of the Federal Reserve System consists of seven members appointed by the President of the United States and confirmed by the Senate. Board members devote their full time to the business of the Board. They are appointed for terms of fourteen years, and their terms are so arranged that one expires every two years. No two members of the Board may come from the same Federal Reserve district.

One of the Board's duties is to supervise the operations of the Federal Reserve System. As already indicated, the Board appoints three of the nine directors of each Federal Reserve Bank, including the chairman and the deputy chairman. And appointments of the president and first vice president of each Federal Reserve Bank are subject to the Board's approval. The Board also issues regulations that interpret and apply the provisions of law relating to Reserve Bank operations. It directs Reserve Bank activities in examination and supervision of banks and coordinates the System's economic research and publications.

Each of the twelve Federal Reserve Banks submits its budget to the Board for approval. The salaries of all officers and employees of the Reserve Banks and branches are subject to the Board's approval. Certain other expenditures—such as those for construction or major alteration of bank buildings—are also subject to the Board's specific approval. The Board's staff analyzes reports showing expenses of the Federal Reserve Banks and also makes surveys at the Reserve Banks of operating procedures and of other matters relating to their expenses and cost accounting systems.

Each Federal Reserve Bank and branch is examined at least once a year by the Board's field examiners, who are directed to determine the financial condition of the Bank and compliance by its management with applicable provisions of law and regulation. The scope of examination includes a comprehensive review of the Bank's expenditures to determine if such expenditures are properly controlled and are of a nature appropriate for a Reserve Bank. It is also the practice to have representatives of a public accounting firm observe the examination of one Reserve Bank each year, to provide an outside evaluation of the adequacy and effectiveness of examination procedures.

In addition to the annual examination by the Board's examiners, the operations of each Reserve Bank are audited by the Bank's internal auditing staff on a year-round basis under the direction of a resident General Auditor. He is responsible to the Bank's board of directors through its chairman and its audit committee. Each year the Board's examiners review thoroughly the internal audit programs at all of the Banks to see that the coverage is adequate and the procedures effective.

THE FEDERAL RESERVE SYSTEM: ORGANIZATION

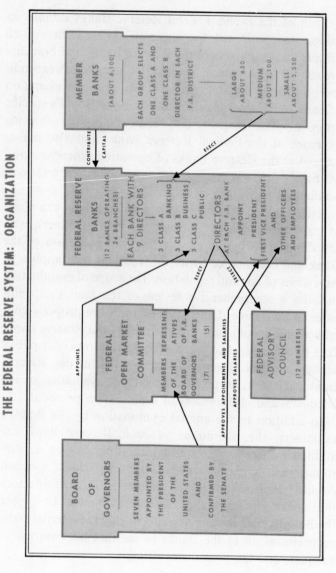

The Board represents the Federal Reserve System in most of its relations with executive departments of the Government and with congressional committees. It is required to exercise special supervision over foreign contacts and international operations of the Reserve Banks.

The Board submits an annual report to Congress and publishes a weekly statement, as described in Chapter XI, of the assets and liabilities of the Federal Reserve Banks. Expenses incurred by the Board in carrying out its duties are paid out of assessments upon the Reserve Banks, and the Board's accounts are audited each year by qualified certified public accountants.

Federal Open Market Committee

Systemwide coordination in the administration of monetary policy is accomplished in part through the Federal Open Market Committee, a statutory body that meets at the Board's offices in Washington at frequent intervals. Its membership comprises the seven members of the Board of Governors and presidents of five of the Federal Reserve Banks. It is assisted by a staff of economists drawn from the staffs of the Board and the Banks. The Committee has responsibility for deciding on changes to be made in the System's portfolio of domestic securities and holdings of foreign currencies. The Federal Reserve Banks, in their operations in the open market, are required by law to carry out the decisions of the Open Market Committee.

Federal Advisory Council

To establish a further link and channel of communication between the Board and representatives of the banking

THE FEDERAL RESERVE SYSTEM

and business community, the Federal Reserve Act provides for a Federal Advisory Council consisting of one member from each Federal Reserve district. Each Federal Reserve Bank by its board of directors annually selects one Council member, usually a representative banker in its district. The Council meets in Washington at least four times a year. It confers with the Board of Governors on business conditions and makes advisory recommendations regarding the affairs of the Federal Reserve System.

Other Advisory Committees

In dealing with the many operating and functional problems that call for a coordinated approach and solution to make a decentralized system effective, the System makes use of a number of conferences and committees that help in reaching an understanding on common problems. Of these the most important are the Conference of Presidents and the Conference of Chairmen of the Federal Reserve Banks. The former Conference meets at least three times a year, while the latter usually meets once a year, at the Board's offices in Washington.

Membership in the Federal Reserve System

The blending of private and public, and regional and national, interests in the Federal Reserve System has created an organization especially well adapted to a dynamic, private enterprise economy such as ours and to a banking system with many independent banks. On June 30, 1963, the Federal Reserve System had 6,058 member banks out of a total of 13,993 banks in the country. Of those that were members, 4,537 were national banks, which are required to belong to the System, and

24

1,521 were State-chartered banks. Banks with State charters may join the System if qualified for membership and if accepted by the Federal Reserve.

While somewhat less than one-half of the banks in the United States belonged to the System on June 30, 1963, these banks held nearly three-fourths of the country's total bank deposits. Furthermore, they held about 85 per cent of all demand deposits, which, along with currency, serve as means of payment. Consequently, Federal Reserve policies have a direct influence on institutions holding nearly nine-tenths of the bank deposits that constitute the major component of the country's money supply.

The different kinds of banks in this country in mid-1963 and the amounts of their demand and time deposits are shown in the accompanying table.

BANKS IN THE UNITED STATES, JUNE 30, 1963

Kind of bank	Number	Deposits [1] (in millions of dollars)	
		Demand	Time
Member bank [2]...................	6,058	121,308	86,550
Nonmember bank................	7,935	23,705	62,271
Total......................	13,993	145,013	148,820
Classes of member banks:			
National [2].....................	4,537	78,425	58,462
State........................	1,521	42,884	28,088
Classes of nonmember banks:			
Commercial...................	7,424	23,376	19,353
Mutual savings................	511	330	42,918

[1] Excludes interbank deposits.
[2] Includes one national (member) bank in the Virgin Islands.
NOTE.—Details may not add to totals because of rounding.

25

Obligations and Privileges of Member Banks

When banks join the Federal Reserve System, they become eligible to use all of the System's facilities. At the same time they undertake to abide by certain rules, prescribed by law or developed by regulation in accordance with the law, for the protection of the public interest.

National banks are chartered by the Comptroller of the Currency, a Federal Government official, and are subject in their operations to the National Bank Act as well as to the Federal Reserve Act. State-chartered banks that become members of the Federal Reserve System retain their charter privileges but agree to be subject to the requirements of the Federal Reserve Act. Since these banks join the System voluntarily, they have the privilege of withdrawing from membership on six months' notice.

Every member bank is required to subscribe to the capital of its Reserve Bank. Its paid-in subscription is an amount equal to 3 per cent of its capital and surplus, and another 3 per cent is subject to call. On June 30, 1963, all member banks together held about $480 million of paid-in capital stock of the twelve Federal Reserve Banks.

Banks that become members of the Federal Reserve System must assume several important obligations. They must maintain legally required reserves either on deposit without interest at the Reserve Bank or as cash held in their own vaults; remit at par for checks drawn against them when presented by a Reserve Bank for payment; and comply with various Federal laws, regulations, and conditions of membership regarding the adequacy of capital, mergers with other banking institutions, establishment of branches, relations with holding company affiliates and

26

bank holding companies, interlocking directorates, loan and investment limitations, and other matters. If the member bank is chartered by a State, it must be subject to general supervision and examination by the Federal Reserve System.

In return, member banks are entitled to the following principal privileges, among others: (1) to borrow from the Federal Reserve Banks when temporarily in need of additional funds, subject to criteria for such borrowing (customarily called discounting) set by statute and regulation; (2) to use Federal Reserve facilities for collecting checks, settling clearing balances, and transferring funds to other cities; (3) to obtain currency whenever required; (4) to share in the informational facilities provided by the System; (5) to participate in the election of six of the nine directors of the Federal Reserve Bank for their district; and (6) to receive a cumulative statutory dividend of 6 per cent on the paid-in capital stock of the Federal Reserve Bank.

Use of these privileges by member banks throughout the country enables the nation's banking system to operate more effectively in providing the credit and banking facilities needed in a growing and diverse economy.

CHAPTER III

INSTRUMENTS OF MONETARY REGULATION. *The principal means by which monetary policy achieves its objectives are open market purchases and sales, mainly of U. S. Government securities but also of foreign currencies; discount operations; and changes in reserve requirements. Regulation of stock market credit supplements these means of influence. Use of all the instruments is closely coordinated.*

FEDERAL Reserve monetary policy is exercised principally through three related and complementary instruments affecting the reserve position of the banking system. These are open market operations in domestic securities, discount operations, and changes in reserve requirements. Open market operations in foreign currencies also affect bank reserve positions to some extent, but their focus is on orderly achievement of balance in the supply of and demand for dollars in the foreign exchange market.

Changes in bank reserves result in a multiple expansion or contraction of bank loans and investments and of the money supply, as explained in some detail in the next chapter. The lending and investment activities of banks in turn influence conditions in the nation's credit market. Thus, actions by the Federal Reserve System to create or extinguish bank reserves not only exert a powerful influence on the flow of bank credit and money but also have a marginal influence on the levels of interest rates and on liquidity and the availability of credit in general.

In addition to its use of general monetary policy instruments to affect bank reserves, the Federal Reserve has authority to influence directly the volume of stock market credit. This limited-purpose instrument is specially designed to prevent the excessive use of bank and other credit in stock market speculation.

The timing and degree of the use of these Federal Reserve instruments and their coordination are of major importance in making credit and monetary policy effective in relation to domestic economic conditions and our international balance of payments.

OPEN MARKET OPERATIONS

The bulk of Federal Reserve operations affecting the reserve positions of banks relate to short-term variations in the economy's needs for bank credit and are effected by the use of open market operations. These operations consist of purchases or sales of securities in the open market. Regardless of who may sell the securities purchased or who may buy the securities sold by the Federal Reserve, these transactions have a direct impact on the volume of member bank reserves. A distinctive aspect of open market operations is that they are undertaken solely on the initiative of the Federal Reserve.

How Operations Are Conducted

Open market purchases or sales of securities are made by the Manager of the System's Open Market Account under instruction of the Federal Open Market Committee, which is responsible for making the open market decisions of the entire System. Open market transactions are in U.S. Government securities primarily, but sometimes they include relatively small amounts of bankers' acceptances. The purchases or sales of foreign currencies, when required by the economy's external position, are also under the direction of this Committee.

The System Open Market Account buys securities from or sells securities to dealers, who transact orders for their own account as well as for others. Purchases for the Open Market Account are made at the lowest prices, and sales at the highest prices, that are available in the market at the time of the transaction.

When the Federal Open Market Account buys securities in the open market, the dealer receives a check on a Reserve Bank in payment, which he deposits in his own bank account. When a member bank receives these funds, they are credited to its reserve account with a Reserve Bank. Federal Reserve purchases of securities thus add to the reserve balances of member banks. Conversely, sales of securities reduce the reserve balances of member banks. The resulting changes in reserve positions affect the ability of these banks to make loans and to buy securities.

Federal Reserve open market sales are made outright. Purchases, on the other hand, may be outright or under repurchase agreement. When such agreements are made, the selling dealer agrees to repurchase the securities within a specified period of fifteen days or less. This kind of

31

arrangement provides Federal Reserve credit on a temporary basis — puts out the funds with a string tied to them, as it were. It also provides temporary financing of dealer inventories at a time when funds for dealer loans are not readily available in the market and the System is willing to supply bank reserves for a limited period. Repurchase agreements may be terminated before maturity at the option of either party.

Open Market Procedures

The effectuation of credit and monetary policy has been the principal objective of open market operations since the early 1950's. For several years before World War II and for a few years thereafter, however, maintenance of orderly conditions in the money and securities markets was officially declared to be a main purpose of System open market operations. During the period of war and early postwar finance, orderliness became extended to include stability of market prices and yields. Thus, the Federal Reserve bought and sold Government securities with the purpose of stabilizing prices and yields. As a result, all Government securities — whether short-term or long-term — could be converted into cash with equal ease. In other words, all Government securities had full market liquidity.

This experience demonstrated that use of open market operations to stabilize market prices and yields of Government securities prevents the System from regulating bank reserves in the interest of the whole economy. When offerings of securities in the market exceeded the private demand for them, the Federal Reserve was obliged to buy them to keep the market stable. As a result, commercial bank reserves were expanded automatically, even at times when such expansion was adverse to the public interest. By functioning as residual buyer, the System created bank reserves mainly at the initiative of the market rather than on its own initiative.

This operating dilemma came into sharp focus when the Korean crisis in 1950 caused a rapid increase in credit demands and a surge of inflationary pressures. To resolve the dilemma, an accord was reached with the Treasury early in 1951 that the Federal Reserve System would discontinue stabilizing prices and yields of Government securities. Following this accord, the Federal Open Market Committee was able to conduct open market operations with the principal objective of implementing credit and monetary policy, including the correction of disorderly market situations should any occur.

The Open Market Committee has always followed a policy of reviewing and reaffirming or changing its established operating procedures each year, or whenever necessary. Changes in procedure have been made over the years, as economic conditions have changed. Over most of the 1950's, for instance, when the U.S. balance of payments was not a principal concern, practically all emphasis was placed on domestic economic conditions. In the early 1960's the balance of payments became a more pressing problem, and open market operations and procedures came to reflect this. For instance, the Open Market Committee began to operate regularly in U.S. Government securities of all maturities in order to have a more direct effect on interest rates, especially short-term rates, which have an influence on the flow of liquid funds between the United States and foreign countries.

While operating procedures have changed from time to time over the years since 1951, the basic position of the System in relation to the Treasury or to the Government securities market has always included the following major elements. First, effectuation of credit and monetary policy has been the principal objective of open market operations, although correction of disorderly market conditions has been necessary at times. Second, decisions about operations in particular securities have been made in the light of economic and financial circumstances, although the bulk of open market operations have been in short-term securities because they have the largest market and because transactions can be consummated without undue market disturbance. And third, the System has undertaken no operations to peg U.S. Government securities or to create artificial market conditions at times of new security offerings by the Treasury. At the same time it has tried not to introduce substantial changes in Federal Reserve policy during financing periods.

Effectuation of policy. Open market operations are administered so as to affect bank reserve positions, and thereby the flow of bank credit and money. As with other domestic policy instruments, they are used to help minimize short-term fluctuations in economic activity, to facilitate the expansion of money and credit necessary to continuing economic growth, and to help maintain relative stability in average prices of goods and services.

The efficient conduct of open market operations requires a well performing Government securities market. In such a market, prices and yields at which willing buyers and willing sellers can arrange transfers of ownership are continuously being established. These prices and yields affect the allocation of funds within the market and between it and other markets and uses. It is important that operations of monetary policy be designed so that the process of providing bank reserves interferes with basic market functions as little as possible.

The credit market, however, does not always function effectively and well. It sometimes reflects unusual psychological tensions growing out of overly optimistic or overly pessimistic expectations as to some prospective development, economic or political and domestic or international. Monetary policy must be responsive to such destabilizing developments and counteract them when they occur.

Market disturbances are usually limited in extent, and the self-correcting tendencies characteristic of a sensitive market mechanism keep the flow of trading continuous and orderly. There is always a possibility, however, that a market disturbance will become self-feeding and that the market situation will become disorderly. Under these circumstances, the System undertakes open market transactions to correct disorderly conditions.

Security operations. In its day-to-day operations the System relies on open market operations as its most sensitive and flexible instrument for affecting bank reserves. The System is continuously buying and selling securities in the open market as it accommodates seasonal demands for money and credit, attempts to offset cyclical economic swings, and supplies the bank reserves needed for long-term growth. The net change in its securities portfolio tends to be comparatively small over, say, a year, but over the same period the System undertakes a large volume of transactions — purchases and sales together — in response to seasonal and other temporary variations in

35

reserve availability that might otherwise lead to undesirable market instabilities.

To minimize the direct impact on markets of continual and sizable day-to-day purchases and sales, much the larger part of open market operations are carried out in short-term securities. But operations have also been undertaken, when appropriate, in intermediate- and long-term securities. These have been purchased at times to take immediate downward pressure off short-term rates in order to discourage outflows of liquid capital from the United States and thereby to help our balance of payments, while still encouraging domestic credit expansion.

GOVERNMENT SECURITY TRANSACTIONS, 1962

	MATURITY CLASS		
	Within 1 year	1 - 5 years	Over 5 years
	Billions of dollars		
ALL TRANSACTIONS	244	34	24
FEDERAL RESERVE OPEN MARKET	15	2	*

* Less than $0.5 billion.   NOTE.—Excludes transactions among U.S. Government securities dealers and also Federal Reserve exchanges, redemptions, and repurchase agreements.

In 1962, System open market transactions in securities maturing within a year amounted to $15 billion, while transactions in maturities of one to five years were about $2 billion, and in longer-term securities less than $0.5 billion. As can be seen from the table on the preceding page, over-all activity in the market also declined as maturity lengthened.

Experience shows that changes in commercial bank reserve positions brought about by System open market operations, whether in short- or long-term securities, do affect the entire Government securities market and also the market for other securities in some degree. Many institutional investors, especially commercial banks and savings institutions, hold securities of longer term along with some of shorter term. In adapting the maturity distribution of their portfolios to their special needs, the managers of these portfolios are necessarily alert and sensitive to changes in demand and supply in the market and are continuously adjusting their portfolios as they assess and reassess prospects for the market. Thus they adapt their portfolios to changing market conditions and in this process transmit the effects of Federal Reserve operations throughout the range of maturities of debt obligations outstanding.

Periods of Treasury financing. During the period of World War II and through early postwar years, when the Federal Reserve System was stabilizing the market, it purposely used its open market instrument to support Treasury borrowing operations. To this end the System engaged in open market transactions in maturing issues, in securities announced for issuance ("when issued" securities), and in outstanding issues of maturities comparable to those being offered by the Treasury in a par-

37

ticular refinancing. With its virtually unlimited resources, the System competed with market traders in such transactions and the latter, in consequence of the System's dominant role in the market, tended to limit the volume of their own trading.

The risk to System policy from this situation was not only the undesired release to the banks during Treasury financings of additional reserve funds but also the interference, when not necessarily warranted, with the process by which the market allocates funds among competing users. In order to avoid or limit this risk, the System discontinued this kind of operation in 1953. Discontinuance of the practice of facilitating Treasury borrowings also had as a broad objective the fostering of a more self-reliant Government securities market.

This action, however, could not resolve all aspects of the market relationship between debt management and monetary administration. The marketable and convertible part of the Federal debt held by the public at the end of 1962 amounted to more than $160 billion. The periodic refinancing of this debt and the need from time to time for new cash borrowing require that the Treasury engage frequently in financing operations, other than its weekly auctions of Treasury bills. While the System has believed that its powers to create money should not be used to support these financings, it has recognized that concurrent monetary actions may affect their success. Consequently, the Federal Reserve has come to pursue whenever feasible what is known as an "even keel" monetary policy immediately before, during, and immediately after Treasury financing operations.

Maintenance of an "even keel" in monetary management during Treasury financing periods helps to keep abrupt changes in bank credit conditions from interfering with Treasury financings. It has the disadvantage of shifting to periods before or after such financings whatever changes in monetary action may be appropriate in the prevailing economic situation from the standpoint of the public interest. These shifts in the timing of action, however, are not frequent and in any event can be accomplished without destabilizing effects upon the economy.

Foreign currency operations. In early 1962 the Federal Reserve began to buy and sell foreign currencies for the Open Market Account in the exchange markets and in direct transactions with foreign monetary authorities. These operations in foreign currencies are especially related to the state of balance in the international payments of the United States and hence need to be considered in connection with that subject, as is done in Chapter VIII. It may be noted here that such operations help to retard outflows of gold from this country during periods of payment deficits and to fortify the dollar in foreign exchange markets during periods of actual or potential speculative pressure.

Foreign currency transactions by the Federal Reserve do have an effect on domestic bank reserves, but in view of the actual size and nature of operations the net effect is quite small. Sales of foreign currencies, like sales of U.S. Government securities, absorb reserves, while acquisitions of such currencies add to reserves. In deciding on the extent of day-to-day open market operations in U.S. Government securities, the System of course takes into account the effect of these operations and of all other factors affecting bank reserves.

DISCOUNT OPERATIONS

An important advantage to a commercial bank of being a member of the Federal Reserve System is that it may obtain additional reserves on occasion by borrowing from a Federal Reserve Bank. As a matter of fact, provision of facilities for such borrowing was a main objective of reserve banking as established in this country.

Mechanics of Discounting

Member banks may borrow from a Reserve Bank in two ways. First, they may rediscount short-term commercial, industrial, agricultural, or other business paper, with recourse on the borrowing bank. Second, they may give their own promissory notes secured by paper eligible for discounting, by Government securities, or by other satisfactory collateral. Borrowings by the first method are called discounts; by the latter, advances. The custom has developed of referring to both types of Reserve Bank lending as discounting, and the interest charge applicable to such lending is known as the discount rate.

Actually, most member bank borrowing has come to be in the form of advances — that is, against notes with Government securities as collateral. This form of borrowing is more convenient and time-saving for the bank, because the collateral is free of credit risk, is instantly appraisable as to value, and can be more readily supplied in large amounts conforming to the borrowing needs of individual banks. Many member banks leave Government securities with their Reserve Bank for safekeeping; this arrangement makes it easy to pledge such securities as collateral when they need to borrow.

When a member bank borrows at a Reserve Bank, the proceeds of the loan are added or credited to its reserve balance on deposit at the Reserve Bank. Conversely, when it repays its indebtedness, the amount of repayment is deducted from or charged against its reserve balance. Federal Reserve advances to or discounts for member banks are usually of short maturity — up to fifteen days.

From the viewpoint of the individual member bank, a decision to discount is usually prompted by the need to avoid a deficiency in its legal reserve. Such a deficiency is likely to result from a loss of deposits and therefore of reserves to another bank. In adjusting to such a reserve drain, an individual bank has a number of alternatives. It can restrict its lending, call in correspondent balances it keeps with other banks, sell securities in the market, borrow from another member bank, or borrow from a Reserve Bank.

These alternatives are not equally desirable or possible for all member banks. For instance, a member bank will seek to preserve continuity in providing credit to customers, so it is more likely at first to choose other methods of reserve adjustment. The alternative of calling in correspondent balances is open mainly to smaller banks, which keep such balances with large city banks. Use of this method is limited, though, since banks generally keep these balances above some minimum level in return for services provided by the correspondent bank. Of the remaining methods of reserve adjustment mentioned — selling securities and borrowing from another bank or from the Federal Reserve — the bank will choose borrowing from a Federal Reserve Bank when this method is cheaper or when it seems advantageous for other reasons.

41

Described in this way, the discount facilities of the Reserve Banks would appear to be mainly a convenience to member banks that enables them to adjust their reserve positions to unexpected shifts in deposits by temporary borrowing rather than by an alternative type of adjustment. From the standpoint of the amount of reserve funds available to the banking system, however, borrowing from Reserve Banks is clearly more than a convenience.

Apart from offsetting influences, any increase in Reserve Bank discounts for member banks adds to the total reserves of member banks, and any reduction in the volume of such discounts reduces them. In contrast, when banks that experience reserve drains make their adjustments by selling assets in the market or by interbank borrowing, there may be no effect on total bank reserves. The reserve funds acquired by the banks that are adjusting their reserves may then come from the reserves of other banks.

Discount Administration

Federal Reserve Banks do not discount eligible paper or make advances to member banks automatically. The discount facilities are made available as a privilege of membership in the System and not as a right. Although actual discount operations focus mainly on the temporary financing needs of banks in the normal course of their business, the statutory and regulatory provisions also cover the needs of banks confronted with an emergency situation. The broad discretion that Reserve Banks have in determining satisfactory collateral facilitates borrowing by banks to adjust to exceptional drains on reserves.

Under Regulation A of the Board of Governors, applicable to the discount process, each Federal Reserve Bank in accommodating member bank applications for discount credit adheres to the following guiding principles:

Federal Reserve credit is generally extended on a short-term basis to a member bank in order to enable it to adjust its asset position when necessary because of developments such as a sudden withdrawal of deposits or seasonal requirements for credit beyond those which can reasonably be met by use of the bank's own resources. Federal Reserve credit is also available for longer periods when necessary in order to assist member banks in meeting unusual situations, such as may result from national, regional, or local difficulties or from exceptional circumstances involving only particular member banks. Under ordinary conditions, the continuous use of Federal Reserve credit by a member bank over a considerable period of time is not regarded as appropriate.

In considering a request for credit accommodation, each Federal Reserve Bank gives due regard to the purpose of the credit and to its probable effects upon the maintenance of sound credit conditions, both as to the individual institution and the economy generally. It keeps informed of and takes into account the general character and amount of the loans and investments of the member banks. It considers whether the bank is borrowing principally for the purpose of obtaining a tax advantage or profiting from rate differentials and whether the bank is extending an undue amount of credit for the speculative carrying of or trading in securities, real estate, or commodities, or otherwise.

Member Bank Reluctance to Borrow

The Federal Reserve policy of emphasizing to member banks that the use of its discount facilities should be temporary is reinforced, in practice, by a well established tradition among this country's banks against operating on the basis of borrowed reserves — at least, for any extended period. This tradition does not mean that member banks feel reluctant to rely on Federal Reserve lending facilities to meet temporary or unusual cash drains. But it does mean that under normal conditions these banks manage their affairs so that they do not need to resort to Reserve Bank borrowing except for necessary contingencies. And once in debt, they seek to repay such debt promptly. Continuing pressures on their reserve positions and other special developments may, at times, weaken this reluctance to borrow, but it nonetheless persists as a factor affecting member bank borrowing.

Member bank attitudes toward operating with borrowed funds vary from bank to bank. Many banks never borrow from a Reserve Bank. They prefer to make reserve adjustments in other ways, including, when necessary, restriction of their lending to customers. Reluctance to borrow, as well as incentive to repay promptly, results from the disposition of depositors, especially larger business and financial depositors, to be critical of bank borrowing since, in case of insolvency, creditors' claims take precedence over the claims of depositors.

Because of the tradition against borrowing — and because the Federal Reserve does not consider the continuous use of the discount window by member banks to be appropriate — banks indebted to a Reserve Bank tend to retire this indebtedness from the funds that become available to them before adding to their loans and investments. The act of repayment by one bank is likely to reflect net transfers of reserve funds to that bank from other banks, which may then borrow to replenish their reserve balances and so in turn will need to repay their borrowing. In this way the restrictive effect of member bank indebtedness on their lending tends to spread through the whole banking system. Experience generally shows that tightness in the availability of bank credit to customers is related to a large volume of member bank discounts outstanding, and easy credit conditions to a small volume of borrowing from Reserve Banks.

Discount Rates

Discount rates are the cost to member banks of reserve funds obtained by borrowing from Reserve Banks. Each Reserve Bank must establish its own discount rate, subject to review and determination by the Board of Governors in Washington, every fourteen days. These rates are publicly announced.

The financial community thinks of Reserve Bank discount rates as pivotal rates in the credit market. The key role assigned to them derives largely from the fact that they have been established by the administrative action of a public body having special information and competence to judge whether expansion of bank credit and money is consistent with the economy's over-all cash needs for transactions and liquidity. In the light of this fact, it is only natural that the business and financial community should commonly interpret a change in the level of Reserve Bank discount rates as an important indication of the trend in Federal Reserve policy.

There are no simple rules for interpreting changes in discount rates, however. In general, changes in the discount rate tend to occur when short-term rates of interest in the market have moved away from alignment with the existing discount rate considered to be consistent with the posture of monetary policy and economic circumstances at the time. In some situations, the change represents

45

merely a technical adjustment of discount rates to a shift in market rates stemming from forces that are largely independent of System policy. In other circumstances, earlier action by the System to affect bank reserve availability may have been an influence on the movement of market rates. Adjustment of the discount rate then becomes necessary to assure that the discount mechanism will function effectively in line with current policy. In some periods — and depending on the changes then occurring in economic activity — the level of discount rates may be changed several times in fairly close succession.

Tendency Toward Uniform Rates

The founders of the Federal Reserve System contemplated that Reserve Bank discount rates would be set in accordance with regional financial conditions. They expected that variations in regional conditions would lead to variations in discount rates among the Reserve Banks. In recent decades, however, rates have tended to be uniform, although there have been temporary periods in which different rates have obtained. Basically, this tendency toward uniformity reflects improvements in the facilities and speed of communication and transport as well as further geographical integration of industrial, commercial, and financial enterprise.

Credit is a fluid resource. It tends to flow to the market of highest yield. Along with growth in widely known regional or national enterprises, which can seek financing in the most advantageous market, demands for funds too have become more mobile. The highly sensitive central money markets — that is, the markets for Treasury bills and other prime short-term instruments — provide a mechanism through which the forces of fluid supply and mobile demand are registered promptly.

Thus, the regional credit and money markets have really become only segments of a closely knit national market, as will be explained in Chapter V, and this fact has found expression in a tendency toward uniformity of discount rates among the twelve Reserve Banks. Increasingly, Federal Reserve discount rate policy is referred to and considered in terms of "the discount rate" rather than in terms of twelve Reserve Bank rates.

Relation of the Discount Rate to Market Rates

The level of the discount rate in relation to market rates of interest affects a member bank's decision as to the most desirable way for it to make an immediate adjustment in its reserve position. The cost of adjusting a reserve position by borrowing is, of course, the interest charge incurred. When a bank sells securities to acquire funds, it measures the cost by the interest earnings sacrificed. Thus, a bank's preference as among Federal Reserve discounting, borrowing from other banks, or selling securities is influenced to a large extent by the relation of the discount rate to the cost of borrowing from banks and to market yields on Treasury bills and other securities it holds as liquid assets or as a second line of reserves.

As the chart on page 48 shows, the movement of the Federal Reserve discount rate is closely related to the movement of short-term market interest rates. In a period when credit demands are expanding strongly, short-term market rates tend to rise. One reason for the rise is that when their loans expand rapidly banks sell Treasury bills and other paper of ready marketability to obtain funds.

47

If short-term market rates rise above the discount rate, member banks have a greater tendency to borrow at Reserve Banks rather than to adjust their reserve positions by sale of their liquid paper through the market. Sooner or later under these circumstances, the Reserve Banks are

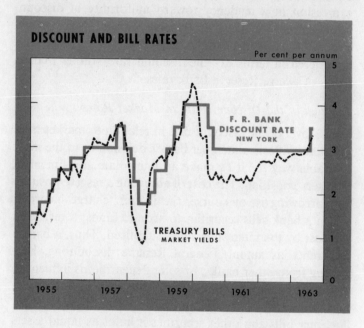

likely to raise the discount rate in order to keep the discount mechanism functioning as a deterrent to unduly rapid expansion of bank credit. Failure to raise the discount rate, in other words, would encourage and enlarge member bank use of the discount window.

On the other hand, if the discount rate is raised above market rates, member banks are likely to prefer to adjust their reserves by selling Government securities, because the cost would be less. But such sales, by increasing the market supply of short-term securities relative to the demand, tend to drive short-term interest rates up toward or moderately above the discount rate. Thus, in a period of strong credit demands, short-term market rates and the discount rate are likely to rise in fairly close sequence until the demand pressures have spent their force.

Federal Funds Rate

In a banking system with as many independent units and with as widely varying banking conditions as prevail in this country, individual banks will at times be deficient in reserves while other banks will have excess reserves. Since total reserve funds are limited in supply, a practice has developed whereby banks with reserve balances in excess of needs offer to lend them on a day-to-day basis to banks deficient in reserves. Thus, in addition to borrowing at Federal Reserve Banks or selling securities in the market, commercial banks may adjust their reserve positions by borrowing from other banks in a fairly well organized market known as the Federal funds market. Banks are the principal participants in this market, but U.S. Government security dealers and others also borrow and lend in the market from time to time.

The interest rate on Federal funds fluctuates in response to the supply of and demand for bank reserves, but it very seldom rises above the discount rate. In fact, the discount rate acts as a kind of ceiling for the Federal funds rate, since member banks naturally prefer discounting if this is less costly.

Conditions of supply and demand in the Federal funds market, which tend to vary directly with general credit conditions, influence member bank borrowing from the Reserve Banks. When general credit conditions are easy, for example, Federal funds are usually available in greater volume than when conditions are tight, and the margin of the Federal funds rate below the discount rate widens. In these circumstances, use of the discount facility by member banks is reduced.

CHANGES IN RESERVE REQUIREMENTS

Federal Reserve authority to vary the required reserve percentages was first made available on a temporary basis in the emergency banking legislation of 1933 and was made a permanent instrument of reserve banking by the Banking Act of 1935. Under present law, the Board of Governors may set within specified limits the required reserve percentages for each of the two classes of member banks — reserve city banks and other banks, which are usually referred to as country banks.

Changes in requirements may be applied to one or both classes of banks at the same time, but they must be kept within the limits set for each class and must be uniform for all banks within a class. The following table shows for each class the range of Federal Reserve discretion over reserve percentages and the percentage requirements in effect in December 1963 and the number of member banks and the distribution of their deposits in mid-1963.

Operation of the Instrument

Action to change the level of reserve requirements does not itself affect the amount of total member bank reserve balances, but it does affect the amount of deposits and of loans and investments that member banks can legally

50

maintain on the basis of a given amount of reserves. As explained in Chapter IV, a given amount of member bank reserves can support more or less bank credit and money depending on the level of required reserve percentages.

MEMBER BANK RESERVE REQUIREMENTS, DECEMBER 1, 1963

Item	Class of bank	
	Reserve city	Other
	Net demand deposits	
Reserve requirements (per cent of deposits):		
Statutory range........................	10 to 22	7 to 14
In effect............................	16½	12
Deposits (percentage distribution, June 30)..	62	38
	Time deposits	
Reserve requirements (per cent of deposits):		
Statutory range........................	3 to 6	3 to 6
In effect............................	4	4
Deposits (percentage distribution, June 30)..	55	45
Number of member banks (June 30).......	219	5,839

Two things happen when required reserve percentages are changed. First, there is an immediate change in the liquid asset or secondary reserve position of member banks. If reserve percentages are raised, banks that do not have enough excess reserves to cover the increase in requirements must find additional reserve funds by selling liquid assets in the market or by borrowing from other banks or from the Reserve Banks; the banking system as a whole, however, can obtain the additional reserve funds required only if the Federal Reserve provides them through its open market operations or if member banks borrow at Reserve Banks.

If reserve percentages are lowered, individual banks find themselves with excess reserves available for investment in earning assets and for debt repayment. Since banks sustain their earnings at the highest levels consistent with solvency by keeping their own resources as fully invested as possible and by avoiding debt, their usual response to a lowering of reserve requirements — after retiring any indebtedness — is to acquire earning assets. At first, they are likely to purchase short-term market paper of high liquidity to hold temporarily.

A second effect of a change in the required reserve percentages is an immediate change in the deposit-expansion-multiplier for the entire banking system. If the required reserve percentage is 20 per cent, $1 of reserves will support $5 of deposits, but if it is reduced to 15 per cent, $1 of reserves will support $6.67 of deposits, as Chapter IV explains in detail. Thus a 15 per cent requirement will support one-third more deposits than a 20 per cent requirement. In practice, the effect of a change in required reserve percentages on the deposit-expansion-multiplier depends in part on the distribution of deposits by type — demand or time and savings — and on the distribution of deposits by class of bank.

Role of Reserve Requirement Changes

As an instrument of monetary management, changes in required reserve percentages are less flexible and continuously adaptable than the open market and discount instruments. For one thing, changes in reserve requirements affect at the same time and to the same extent all member banks subject to the action, regardless of the reserve needs of individual banks on the occasion. For another, even a small change in reserve requirements — say, one-half of one percentage point — results in relatively large changes in the total available reserves and in the liquidity position of member banks as a group. If, to avoid a large reserve effect, a change is limited to a particular class of bank, this raises a perplexing problem of equity as between classes of banks.

Moreover, a change to a new level of reserve requirements cannot be made gradually over a period of time, but must become effective on a selected preannounced date. The credit market is forewarned that on this date either demand or supply pressures will be accentuated, with the risk of disturbance and instability in the prices of and yields on securities at the time.

For the individual member bank the required reserve percentage is the basis for current and forward decisions by management concerning composition and maturity of loans and investments. Accordingly, frequent abrupt changes in the required percentage may unduly complicate the task of bank management in a system of many independent banks of diverse size and portfolio structure. Many of these banks, especially smaller "country banks," are inadequately equipped to make prompt adjustment to frequent, even though small, changes in the reserve requirement percentages.

In the System's experience, changes in reserve requirements have been applied most advantageously in meeting bank reserve situations that had more than temporary significance — that is, would not require reverse operations in the near future — or that did not require careful probing and adjustments as credit markets and the economy responded. In the 1930's the System increased reserve requirements in order to absorb an unnecessarily large volume of excess bank reserves. In early postwar years it increased the percentages in an attempt to absorb the reserves it had supplied by supporting prices of Government securities. The market effect of these increases, however, was such as to necessitate additional purchases to maintain the support.

Since reestablishment of flexible monetary operations in the early 1950's, the Federal Reserve has reduced reserve requirement percentages in recession periods in order to supply bank reserves simultaneously to all parts of the economy. These counter-recession decreases in requirements were facilitated by the fact that existing levels of reserve requirements were high in relation to past periods and also in relation to the standards for nonmember banks adhered to by many States.

In accordance with legislation enacted in 1959, there were reserve requirement changes in 1960 having mainly a structural objective. These adjustments, which at the time released reserves on balance, were for the purpose of unifying reserve requirements for central reserve city banks (a classification in existence at that time) and reserve city banks and of offsetting in part the effects on reserves of making vault cash eligible for meeting reserve requirements. Before this legislation, member banks were not permitted to count vault cash in meeting their reserve requirements.

In the fall of 1962, in an effort to keep short-term interest rates from falling in view of the balance of payments problem, the Federal Reserve reduced the reserve requirement against time and savings deposits for the first time in eight years. The reduction, which helped to provide reserves for economic growth, was timed so as to accommodate the large seasonal demand for bank credit and money that normally occurs over the holiday period. In addition, it provided the reserves in such a way as to take direct downward pressures off short-term interest rates. In the absence of such a reduction the System would have provided these reserves mainly through open market purchases of short-term securities.

REGULATION OF STOCK MARKET CREDIT

Since 1933 the Federal Reserve has been directed by law to restrain the undue use of bank credit for speculation in securities, real estate, or commodities. Since 1934 the System has been specifically authorized to curb the excessive use of credit for purchasing or carrying securities by setting limitations on the amount that brokers and dealers in securities, banks, and others may lend on securities for that purpose. At brokers and dealers the regulatory limitation applies to any type of corporate security; at banks it applies only to corporate stocks registered on national securities exchanges. The regulatory limitation does not apply to any loan for other purposes, even though stocks may be pledged as collateral for the loan.

The mechanism of stock market credit regulation is readily illustrated. The amount that lenders may advance against securities is always less than the current market value of the securities to be pledged as collateral. The lender calls the difference between the two the customer's margin. For example, if a loan of $6,000 is secured by stock having a market worth of $10,000, the customer's margin is $4,000, or 40 per cent, and the loan value of the stock is 60 per cent of its market value. Thus, by prescribing the loan value of the securities, the customer's margin may be controlled; the less the amount that can be lent, the greater the margin required. In recent years the margin required by Federal Reserve regulation has varied from 90 per cent to 50 per cent.

Federal Reserve regulation requires the lender to obtain the specified margin in connection with the purchase of the security. If the market value of the security that is collateral for the loan subsequently declines, the regulation does not make it necessary for the borrower either to put up additional collateral or to reduce the indebtedness. However, the banker or broker making the loan may require additional collateral if he deems it to be necessary.

If the Federal Reserve raises the margin requirement, borrowers need not reduce existing loans (or increase the amount of collateral deposited with the broker or with the bank), but borrowers with under-margined accounts have to apply half of the proceeds from any sales of the securities they have pledged as collateral to reduce their indebtedness.

Regulation of stock market credit by the margin requirement, though applied through the facilities of the lender, puts restraint on the borrower and thus dampens demand for credit. An important aspect of this restraint is that it limits the amount of pyramiding of borrowing that can take place in a rising market as higher prices create higher collateral values and permit more borrowing on the same collateral.

The purposes of regulation through margin requirements are to minimize the danger of excessive use of credit in financing stock market speculation and to prevent the recurrence of speculative stock market booms based on credit financing, such as culminated in the price collapse of 1929 and the subsequent severe credit liquidation. A stock market boom followed by collapse is always possible, but without excessive feeding by credit-financed speculation it is not likely to assume the proportions or to have the effects that it had in earlier periods.

COORDINATION OF MONETARY INSTRUMENTS

Provision of bank reserves to meet the economy's long-term growth and shorter-term cyclical and seasonal needs is accomplished through coordinated use of the three basic instruments of monetary policy. Reserves provided through open market operations and changes in reserve requirements are at the initiative of the Federal Reserve. On the other hand, reserves provided through discounting or lending to member banks are at the initiative of banks, although use of this initiative is influenced by Federal Reserve actions affecting the discount rate and market conditions.

In the banking system of the United States the great bulk of reserve funds in the possession of banks are non-borrowed reserves. They represent the result of cumulative actions taken in the past at the initiative of reserve banking authorities. Some of these are the results of decisions to supply reserves through use of policy instruments; some, of decisions not to use policy instruments to offset increases in reserves from other sources, such as gold inflows.

Since the early 1930's banks in the United States have generally confined their use of the discount window to meeting temporary needs for reserve funds. Hence in this period the Federal Reserve has provided bank reserves to support long-term growth of the economy in part by open market operations and in part by changes in reserve requirements. It has also changed reserve requirement levels in special situations where large changes in the volume of bank reserves, such as those stemming from unduly large and persistent movements of gold into or out of this country, needed to be offset or cushioned.

In practice, the bulk of day-to-day Federal Reserve operations are in response to the short-term seasonal and cyclical changes in economic and financial conditions. In these circumstances open market operations as a tool of policy are complemented by discount operations. System initiative affecting bank reserves in order to accommodate seasonal needs and to temper cyclical swings in the economy is accomplished mainly through open market operations in U.S. Government securities. But also individual member banks, especially in communities that are subject to unusually wide seasonal or cyclical fluctuations in business payments and credit demands, may cushion or spread out somewhat the reserve adjustments they find it necessary to make through resort to the discount mechanism.

How the Federal Reserve carries out its shorter-term policy adjustments by the joint use of open market and discount policy is a complex process. An important characteristic of the process is that member bank demands for borrowing from Reserve Banks in general tend to vary inversely with the volume of reserves that the System is supplying through open market operations.

When the Federal Reserve curtails reserve funds by open market sales of securities in a period of high and rising economic activity, for example, member banks can accommodate expanding demands for credit only by increased use of the discount window.

To limit incentives for member bank discounting in such periods the System may need to raise the discount rate in

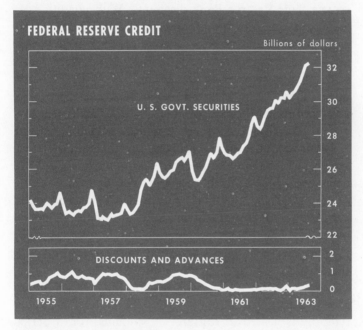

FEDERAL RESERVE CREDIT

Billions of dollars

U. S. GOVT. SECURITIES

DISCOUNTS AND ADVANCES

accordance with changes in the general credit situation and with the increases that are likely to be occurring in market rates of interest. The active use of the open market and discount instruments jointly to slow down the pace of bank credit and monetary expansion will not be extended indefinitely, but only long enough to contain unduly expansive tendencies in these quantities.

Interaction of the open market and discount instruments

is also involved when countercyclical monetary policy is directed toward accelerating the expansion of bank credit and money. If member banks are heavily indebted to the Reserve Banks, they will use the reserve funds made available to them by enlarged open market purchases first to reduce their Reserve Bank discounts. With conditions in credit markets showing progressive ease — reflected especially by declining rates of interest on short-term securities — the discount rate may be lowered in one or more steps. The continued inflow of reserve funds to banks under these conditions will soon result in observable acceleration in the rise of total member bank reserves and in the pace of bank credit and monetary expansion.

In connection with the problem of moderating cyclical swings in the flow of bank credit and money, it should be noted that, in a growing economy, developments seldom call for a full halt in or an all-out stimulation of bank credit expansion. Adaptations in the joint use of the monetary instruments, therefore, are generally gradual, that is, made in greater or lesser degree according to the needs shown by the stream of current economic information. Although in this process day-by-day changes in the availability of reserve funds may vary considerably, monetary policy typically is geared to restraint or stimulus over a period of many months.

The System also makes joint use of monetary instruments as it adapts them to attainment of objectives for both domestic economic activity and the balance of payments. Its open market operations to provide reserves for domestic economic expansion may be associated with downward pressures on interest rates, especially on short-term rates, which in turn may lead to outflows of capital from this country. If these outflows occur at times when they add to deficits in the U.S. balance of payments or threaten to activate large destabilizing speculative pressures, use of the instruments must be jointly adapted to take these outflows into account.

To some extent the System may make open market security purchases in intermediate- or long-term securities to take immediate downward pressures off short-term rates. The Treasury, it should also be mentioned, may at the same time issue short-term securities in an effort to offset downward rate pressures. Meanwhile, the Federal Reserve discount rate may be maintained above market rates; this encourages member banks to cover whatever reserve deficiencies emerge by selling securities, especially short-term issues, and thus puts upward pressure on short-term interest rates. And finally the Federal Reserve may sell foreign currencies to help forestall drains on our gold stock and to reduce associated speculative pressures.

Regulation of stock market credit supplements the instruments affecting the bank reserve base. It deals directly and selectively with the possibility of unstable and undue absorption of bank and other credit in stock market speculation. Since fluctuations in stock market activity correlate generally with those in over-all economic activity, changes in margin requirements tend to be similarly correlated. The availability of the margin requirement instrument means that the more general bank reserve instruments do not have to be specially directed to the avoidance of excessive stock speculation financed on credit. Such use of the general instruments, to be effective, would necessarily run the risk of undesirable, broader effects.

CHAPTER IV

FUNCTION OF BANK RESERVES. *Bank reserves constitute both the legally required basis and the functional basis of bank deposits. Changes in the reserve position of banks, therefore, directly affect the flow of bank credit and money. In carrying out its central responsibility, the Federal Reserve System relies primarily on its ability to increase or decrease the volume and cost of bank reserves.*

MONETARY policy actions initially affect bank reserves. Therefore, it is important — in tracing the impact of monetary policy on the economy — to understand the function of bank reserves and the relation between changes in bank reserves and changes in bank credit and deposits.

Commercial banks, like other businesses, are organized to make a profit. The bulk of a commercial bank's earnings come from the returns it receives on the loans and securities it holds. Hence, it is usually a bank's policy to put into loans and investments as much as possible of the money it receives as capital and deposits. In practically all States, however, such banks are required by law to hold as reserve assets an amount of uninvested funds equal to a designated proportion of their deposits.

Historically, reserve requirements were imposed by law for the purpose of protecting depositors — to assure that banks maintained enough cash to meet temporary drains on reserve funds caused by their depositors' withdrawals as well as to elicit depositors' confidence in the banks' ability to redeem their deposits when called upon to do so. This was before establishment of the Federal Reserve System, when there was no reserve bank from which commercial banks could obtain additional reserves in time of temporary need.

Reserve requirements, although they restrained credit expansion, did not effectively protect depositors during periods of stress, for the banks could not continuously pay out for their depositors' benefit the cash they were required to keep as reserves without drawing such reserves down below legal requirements and threatening their ability to continue active operations. Since other ways of protecting depositors have been developed (for example, insurance of deposits by the Federal Deposit Insurance Corporation), required bank reserves have become for the most part a medium through which the flow of bank credit and money is influenced.

Thus, reserve requirements now serve mainly as a base for monetary regulation. They do this in two ways. First, the existence of reserve requirements enables the Federal Reserve to gauge more accurately than it otherwise could the likely impact on bank credit of operations affecting the availability of bank reserves; in this sense, reserve requirements are a fulcrum for monetary policy. Secondly, the possibility of making changes in reserve requirements, as discussed in Chapter III, provides a means by which the deposit-expansion-multiplier for the banking system can be altered, when desirable, to affect the over-all availability of bank credit and money.

Member Bank Reserve Requirements

Each bank that was a member of the Federal Reserve System as of December 1, 1963, was required to keep as reserves the following percentages of its demand deposits:

Reserve city banks........................... 16½
Other member banks (often described as
    "country banks")........................ 12

These reserves must be on deposit with a Federal Reserve Bank, except for any amounts that the member bank may choose to hold in actual cash. As explained in Chapter III, the Federal Reserve changes the required percentages within the limits specified by law when credit conditions make such a change appropriate and feasible. Banks that are not members of the Federal Reserve System are subject to reserve requirements that vary by State.

The function of bank reserves may be easily explained in a general way. For instance, assume that banks are required to hold a 20 per cent reserve against demand deposits. This 20 per cent figure is higher than the actual percentages given above, but it is a convenient round figure for illustrative purposes.

In this example, when a member bank receives a demand deposit of $100, in currency or in the form of a check on another bank, it must hold $20 as required reserves against the deposit. These reserves must be deposited with a

Federal Reserve Bank, unless held in currency in the bank's own vault. The bank is free to lend or invest the remaining $80. If there is an adequate demand for loans from customers or a supply of suitable securities in the market, the bank will lend or invest practically all of the $80.

How the Banking System Works

To further clarify the role of reserves in the banking system, let us imagine that there is only one commercial bank in the United States, that it is the sole member bank in the Federal Reserve System, and that all of its liabilities to customers are in the form of demand deposits. Furthermore, let us give this single member bank enough resources to represent all the commercial banks in the country. Let us assume that the relevant items in its balance sheet are as follows (in billions):

Loans and investments...................... $ 80
Reserves with the Federal Reserve........... 20
Demand deposits........................... 100
Ratio of reserves to demand deposits......20 per cent

Let us again assume that this 20 per cent ratio of reserves to demand deposits is the legal minimum. Under the circumstances the bank would not be in a position to make any additional loans or investments, for its funds are already in use up to the limit permitted by law.

Now let us assume that the Federal Reserve finds that additional loans are desirable to meet the credit needs of the country, and let us also assume that it purchases $10 billion of securities in the market and pays for them by funds that get credited to the seller's demand deposit account in the member bank and are added to the bank's reserve balance at the Federal Reserve. Then the simplified balance sheet of the bank would be (in billions):

Loans and investments.....................	$ 80
Reserves.................................	30
Demand deposits.........................	110
Ratio of reserves to demand deposits.....27.3 per cent	

The member bank would have a higher ratio of reserves to deposits (27.3 per cent) than is required by law (20 per cent). Therefore, it could make additional loans and investments. A little figuring will show that the bank has the $22 billion of reserves required for its deposits of $110 billion and also has $8 billion of reserves above requirements, or excess reserves.

Let us next assume that the public is eager to get additional money and wants to borrow as much as the member bank will lend; let us assume also that the proceeds of the loans will remain on deposit with the bank. This is not a far-fetched assumption, because borrowers most likely want the money in order to pay other depositors in the bank. While there will be transfers from one deposit account to another, no deposits will be withdrawn from the bank, and the total of deposits will stay at the higher level made possible by the increase in reserves.

Another calculation will show that on the basis of the $8 billion of excess reserves the member bank can add $40 billion to its loans and investments. The bank's balance sheet would then be (in billions):

Loans and investments.....................	$120
Reserves.................................	30
Demand deposits.........................	150
Ratio of reserves to demand deposits......20 per cent	

This simplified picture indicates that a deposit of $10 billion of reserve money with the member bank gave rise to a growth of $40 billion in loans and investments and of $50 billion in demand deposits. The calculation, which leaves out of account many complications, shows what a powerful instrument of monetary regulation reserve banking action can be. It can provide the basis for an increase in the money supply not merely by the amount that it adds to the bank's reserves, but by a multiple of the additional reserves — five times in this example.

Suppose now that there is too much money and that Federal Reserve action reduces the $20 billion of reserves the member bank had in the first place by $5 billion, at the same time lowering deposits by an equal amount. The balance sheet would then read (in billions):

Loans and investments...................... $ 80
Reserves.................................. 15
Demand deposits........................... 95
Ratio of reserves to demand deposits......15.8 per cent

On the basis of a 20 per cent legal reserve requirement, the member bank would be deficient in reserves to the extent of $4 billion. The bank would have to call loans or sell investments, and thus absorb deposits to the extent of five times its deficiency in reserves, that is, by $20 billion. If its depositors repaid $20 billion in loans or repurchased that amount of investments by drawing on their deposits, the result would be (in billions):

Loans and investments...................... $ 60
Reserves.................................. 15
Demand deposits........................... 75
Ratio of reserves to demand deposits.......20 per cent

Once more we see the powerful impact of reserve banking action, this time in the direction of contraction. A reduction of $5 billion in the member bank's reserves can bring about a liquidation of $20 billion in loans and investments and a reduction of $25 billion in demand deposits, or money.

The all-important fact brought out by this discussion is that the Federal Reserve, by adding to or extinguishing the member bank's reserves, can influence the bank to increase or decrease its loans and its demand deposits (the major component of the money supply) by several times the amount added or extinguished. This is why the dollars created by Federal Reserve action that become bank reserves are often called "high-powered" dollars to distinguish them from ordinary deposit dollars.

Other Influences

In the exposition so far we have considered one member bank, large enough to represent all the banks in the country, as doing all the banking business. We have assumed that the bank lends or invests as much money as the law permits, and that this action results in the creation of an equal amount of demand deposits. We have also assumed a reserve requirement of 20 per cent and that all the money lent by the bank will be kept on demand deposit. In practice, however, the public generally withdraws some of the money in currency or transfers some of the money to savings or other time deposits.

The changes that occur from time to time in the public's demand for currency will be described in a later chapter. For this chapter, the main point is that the people's demand for currency is related to the total money supply (currency and demand deposits) held by the public, and that such demand reflects merely the share of the money supply that the public desires to hold in the form of currency. Since currency and demand deposits are interchangeable at the option of the public, the major factor increasing or decreasing the money supply is the loans and investments of commercial banks. It should be noted, however, that currency withdrawals from banks reduce bank reserves dollar for dollar. For this reason, currency withdrawals affect the expansion potential of a given volume of new reserve funds.

The transfer of funds from a demand to a savings or other time deposit reflects the preference of the depositor for an asset that earns interest rather than an asset that earns no return but has immediate usefulness as a means of payment. A time deposit cannot have checks drawn against it, and its conversion into cash is subject to certain limitations.

Commercial banks in this country have both demand and time deposits, and their loans, investments, and reserves form a common pool of assets backing the two kinds of deposits. Whereas member banks must keep reserves of about 15 per cent, on the average, against demand deposits, they are required to keep only 4 per cent against savings and other time deposits. If holders of demand deposits transfer them to time deposits, there is a release of reserve funds from the required reserve category — the difference between 15 per cent and 4 per cent — on the basis of which the bank can expand its loans and investments and its demand deposits. Conversely, if holders of time deposits shift them into demand deposits, the bank finds it necessary to reduce its loans and investments or to obtain additional reserve funds in some other way in order to meet the higher reserve requirements against its demand deposits.

Multiplying Power of Bank Reserves

The process of reserve operation in the imaginary situation in which one member bank does all the banking business may now be translated into the actual and more complex situation in which thousands of member banks make loans and investments and hold deposits.

It has been seen that our hypothetical bank can expand its loans and investments by as much as $40 billion if Federal Reserve action adds $10 billion to its reserves. In practice, of course, there are a great many banks in this country, and no one bank can do that since borrowers may wish to take the money out of the lending bank.

In fact, a borrower is likely to use the demand deposit created by his loan to write checks to pay various people. His banker cannot assume that the funds thus paid out will return to his bank in the form of deposits. Consequently, he does not lend more than he has in reserve funds in excess of requirements; if he did, he might not be able to honor the checks of his other depositors. How, then, can all banks together lend four times as much as they obtain in reserves from the Federal Reserve?

The process by which this happens is simple and understandable. It is illustrated in the following chart and table, which show how deposits are built up as reserve funds are diffused throughout the banking system, and may be sketched as follows: Suppose that new reserve funds of $100 are made available to member banks in a manner that also increases deposits by that amount at one bank. The

71

member bank at which $100 is deposited needs to hold $20 in required reserves, in keeping with our earlier assumption, and it may lend or invest the remaining $80.

Suppose that all the money is lent. The amount lent is first credited to the borrower's deposit account. This money is then paid out at once by the borrower to someone who deposits it at another bank. The cash holdings and newly created deposits of the first bank are thus drawn down and transferred to a second bank.

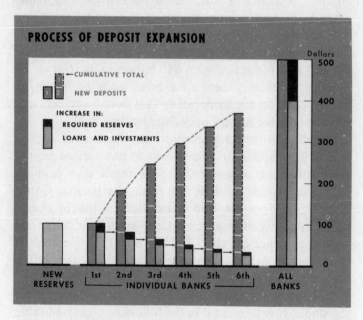

The second bank receives $80 in cash reserves and in new deposits; it holds $16 as required reserve against the deposit received and can lend the remaining $64. Similarly, the borrower here may draw down the additional newly created deposit at once, but the funds will merely be shifted to a third bank, which in turn can lend 80 per cent of $64, thereby adding a further $51.20 to deposits.

This sequence can be traced through many banks until $500 of demand deposits have grown out of the original $100 deposit. On the asset side of their books, the banks hold $100 in reserves (20 per cent of $500) and $400 in loan or investment paper.

MULTIPLYING CAPACITY OF RESERVE MONEY
THROUGH BANK TRANSACTIONS[1]
(In dollars)

Transactions	Deposited in checking accounts	Lent	Set aside as reserves
Bank 1....................	100.00	80.00	20.00
2....................	80.00	64.00	16.00
3....................	64.00	51.20	12.80
4....................	51.20	40.96	10.24
5....................	40.96	32.77	8.19
6....................	32.77	26.22	6.55
7....................	26.22	20.98	5.24
8....................	20.98	16.78	4.20
9....................	16.78	13.42	3.36
10....................	13.42	10.74	2.68
Total for 10 banks......	446.33	357.07	89.26
Additional banks...........	53.67	[2] 42.93	[2] 10.74
Grand total, all banks...	500.00	400.00	100.00

[1] Assuming an average member bank reserve requirement of 20 per cent of demand deposits.
[2] Adjusted to offset rounding in preceding figures.

Thus, an individual bank does not lend more than it receives, but the banking system as a whole expands by a multiple of the new reserve funds made available to it. The fact that individual member banks are required to hold only a fraction of their deposits as reserves and the fact that payments made with the proceeds of bank loans are eventually redeposited with banks make it possible for additional reserve funds, as they are deposited and invested through the banking system as a whole, to generate deposits on a multiple scale.

An Apparent Banking Paradox?

The foregoing discussion of the working of the banking system explains an apparent paradox that is the source of much confusion to banking students. On the one hand, the practical experience of each individual banker is that his ability to make the loans or acquire the investments making up his portfolio of earning assets derives from his receipt of depositors' money. On the other hand, we have seen that the bulk of the deposits now existing have originated through expansion of bank loans or investments by a multiple of the reserve funds available to commercial banks as a group. Expressed another way, increases in their reserve funds are to be thought of as the ultimate source of increases in bank lending and investing power and thus of deposits.

The statements are not contradictory. In one case, the day-to-day aspect of a process is described. In a bank's operating experience, the demand deposits originating in loans and investments move actively from one bank to another in response to money payments in business and personal transactions. The deposits seldom stay with the bank of origin.

The series of transactions is as follows: When a bank makes a loan, it credits the amount to the borrower's deposit account; the depositor writes checks against his account in favor of various of his creditors who deposit them at their banks. Thus the lending bank is likely to retain or receive back as deposits only a small portion of the money that it lent, while a large portion of the money that is lent by other banks is likely to be brought to it by its customers.

From the point of view of the individual bank, therefore, the statement that the ability of a single bank to lend or invest rests largely on the volume of funds brought to it by depositors is correct. Taking the banking system as a whole, however, demand deposits originate in bank loans and investments in accordance with an authorized multiple of bank reserves. The two inferences about the banking process are not in conflict; the first one is drawn from the perspective of one bank among many, while the second has the perspective of banks as a group.

The commercial banks as a whole can create money only if additional reserves are made available to them. The Federal Reserve System is the only instrumentality endowed by law with discretionary power to create (or extinguish) the money that serves as bank reserves or as the public's pocket cash. Thus, the ultimate capability for expanding or reducing the economy's supply of money rests with the Federal Reserve.

New Federal Reserve money, when it is not wanted by the public for hand-to-hand circulation, becomes the reserves of member banks. After it leaves the hands of the first bank acquiring it, as explained above, the new reserve money continues to expand into deposit money as it passes from bank to bank until deposits stand in some established multiple of the additional reserve funds that Federal Reserve action has supplied.

75

How the process of expansion in deposits and bank loans and investments has worked out over the years is depicted by the accompanying chart. The curve "deposits and currency" relates to the public's holdings of demand deposits, time deposits, and currency. Time deposits are included because commercial banks in this country generally engage in both a time deposit and a demand deposit business and do not segregate their loans and investments behind the two types of deposits.

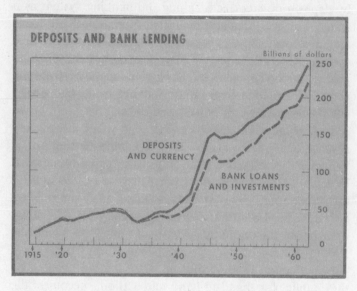

Additional Aspects of Bank Credit Expansion

At this stage of our discussion, three other important aspects of the functioning of the banking system must be noted. The first is that bank credit and monetary expansion on the basis of newly acquired reserves takes place only through a series of banking transactions. Each transaction takes time on the part of individual bank managers and, therefore, the deposit-multiplying effect of new bank reserves is spread over a period. The banking process thus affords some measure of built-in protection against unduly rapid expansion of bank credit should a large additional supply of reserve funds suddenly become available to commercial banks.

The second point is that for expansion of bank credit to take place at all there must be a demand for it by credit-worthy borrowers — those whose financial standing is such as to entail a likelihood that the loan will be repaid at maturity — and/or an available supply of low-risk investment securities such as would be appropriate for banks to purchase. Normally these conditions prevail, but there are times when demand for bank credit is slack, eligible loans or securities are in short supply, and the interest rate on bank investments has fallen with the result that banks have increased their preference for cash. Such conditions tend to slow down bank credit expansion. In general, market conditions for bankable paper and attitudes of bankers with respect to the market exert an important influence on whether, with a given addition to the volume of bank reserves, expansion of bank credit will be faster or slower.

Thirdly, it must be kept in mind that reserve banking power to create or extinguish high-powered money is exercised through a market mechanism. The Federal Reserve may assume the initiative in creating or extinguishing bank reserves, or the member banks may take the initiative through borrowing or repayment of borrowing at the Federal Reserve.

Sometimes the forces of initiative work against one another. At times this counteraction may work to avoid an abrupt impact on the flow of credit and money of pressures working to expand or contract the volume of bank reserves. At other times, banks' desires to borrow may tend to bring about either larger or smaller changes in bank reserves than are desirable from the viewpoint of public policy, especially in periods when banks' willingness to borrow is changing rapidly in response to market forces. The relation between reserve banking initiative and member bank initiative in changing the volume of Federal Reserve credit was discussed in Chapter III.

These additional aspects of bank credit expansion are significant because they indicate that in practice we cannot expect bank credit and money to expand or contract by any simple multiple of changes in bank reserves. Expansion or contraction takes place under given market conditions, and these have an influence on the public's preferences or desires for money and on the banks' preferences for loans and investments. Market conditions are modified in the course of credit expansion or contraction, but the reactions of the public and of the banks will influence the extent and nature of the changes in money and credit that are attained.

Management of Reserve Balances

In managing its reserve balances, an individual commercial bank constantly watches offsetting inflows and outflows of deposits that result from activities of depositors and borrowers. It estimates their net impact on its deposits and its reserve position. Its day-to-day management problem is to make sure that, after all transactions, its reserves are sufficient to comply with legal requirements.

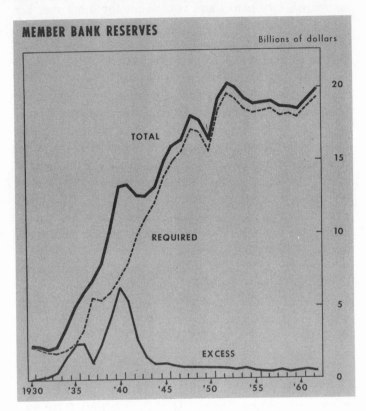

MEMBER BANK RESERVES

Billions of dollars

While a member bank must watch its reserves to make sure that they are large enough, this does not mean that reserves remain unused. Actually, a member bank uses its reserves, most of which are held with the Federal Reserve Bank, in much the same way that a depositor uses his checking account.

79

Under Federal Reserve rules, reserve requirements apply to reserves maintained on the average over a period (a week for reserve city banks and two weeks for other member banks). While maintaining these reserves at or above the required minimum, a bank may make constant use of them. Through its reserve account at its Federal Reserve Bank the bank settles adverse clearing balances with other banks and also transfers funds to other cities. The bank must be careful, however, to see that over the reserve period the average amount of its reserves equals or exceeds the amount required in relation to its deposits. The occasion for borrowing from a Federal Reserve Bank usually arises when reserves have fallen below the required level and banks must replenish them.

At the beginning of this chapter it was stated that banks, as business organizations, endeavor to use all their available funds in profitable ways and keep as reserves only the minimum required by law. During the greater part of the life of the Federal Reserve System, member banks have put practically all their funds to use and have had practically no excess reserves. During the middle and late 1930's and the early part of World War II, however, this was not true as is brought out in the chart on page 79.

After the early 1930's there was a large movement of gold into the country. This gold greatly increased the reserves of member banks. At the same time there was only a limited demand for loans acceptable to banks at current interest rates and a limited supply of investment securities that bankers wanted to acquire at interest rates prevailing in the market. Consequently, the banks had an excessive volume of unused reserves. During and after World War II the greater part of these excess reserves were absorbed into required reserves as credit expanded, demand for currency increased, and increases were made in their reserve requirements, as permitted by law. In recent years excess reserves have once again constituted a relatively small proportion of total reserves, although a larger proportion than in the 1920's.

———————

CHAPTER V

THE CREDIT MARKET. *Commercial banks are part of the national credit market, which is made up of many interrelated markets. Developments in all parts of the market interact on other parts. Neither the banking sector nor the nonbanking sectors of the market can be understood by themselves.*

THE activities of commercial banks — and also the monetary policy actions of the Federal Reserve System — are among the many influences that condition, and are also conditioned by, developments in the national credit market. Through this market the current flow of money saving and of other available funds in the economy is mobilized and invested in loans and securities. These instruments are a representation of, and a means for transferring, the economy's real wealth.

The credit market has many segments, which are differentiated in several ways. Characteristic of the credit transaction — such as the purpose of borrowing and degree of risk involved — is one, and geographic coverage is another. In addition, a variety of financial institutions, businesses, individuals, and governments participate in the market. The commercial banking system plays an important, but in terms of dollar volume by no means the dominant, role in the market, as the chart shows.

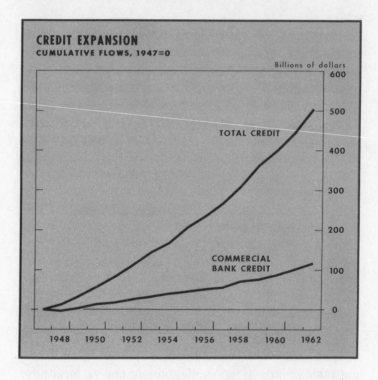

The various parts of the credit market are closely linked. Because of this, developments originating in or affecting the commercial banking system, for example, are soon transmitted to other market institutions and participants. Similarly, market developments appearing initially in other sectors are likely to react soon on banks. Thus, the functions and activities of commercial banks, the Federal Reserve, and other sectors or market participants cannot be understood in isolation.

Nature of the Market

A financial market brings together borrowers and lenders or investors, and it establishes and communicates the prices at which they are willing to make transactions. Some financial markets, such as the stock exchange, are formally organized and have a specific place of business, but most credit markets have no formal organization or designated place of business. Nevertheless, through highly developed mechanisms of communication, they bring together a large number of transactors willing to bid for or offer funds at a price. The price of credit is an interest rate.

Sectors of the credit market differ in several ways. For one, they deal in different kinds of instruments. There are markets for U.S. Government obligations, State and local government obligations, corporate bonds, stocks, bank loans, mortgages on real estate, and so on. Also, the instruments in which they deal vary in maturity, risk, and liquidity; and there are submarkets specializing in securities delineated by these features.

For example, what is commonly known as the "money market" specializes in short-term U.S. Government securities and prime short-term commercial or financial paper. This kind of paper is low in risk and highly liquid, and it typically offers the lowest interest yields. Money market instruments are close substitutes for cash and for each other and are a principal medium for temporary investment by banks, other financial institutions, and business corporations. The term "money market" is often contrasted with the term "capital market," the latter being used to refer to the market for longer-term governmental and private securities.

In practice, however, sharp distinctions between kinds of credit markets are blurred, since markets are all closely

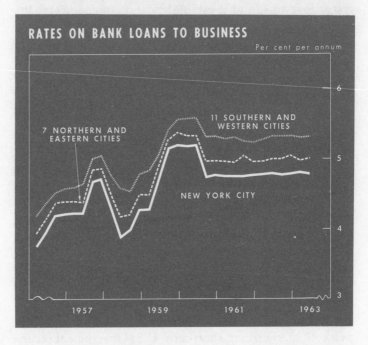

linked through the activities of borrowers, lenders, and investors. As these groups seek the most favorable opportunities for borrowing or for investment of available funds, they find it advantageous to move from one market to another.

The national credit market, geographically, is made up

of a large number of local and regional credit markets. The rates of interest charged and other conditions in these markets may vary, but these rates and markets are nonetheless closely related.

Local and regional credit markets maintain contact with one another in a variety of ways: through the correspondent relations of local banks with banks in other markets; through local contacts with large savings and financing institutions, whose operations may be either regional or national; through arrangements between local dealers in investment securities and either the underwriting houses or members of stock exchanges in the financial centers; and through the facilities of the Federal Reserve System.

Local markets handle for the most part the demand for relatively small loans arising from local needs and based on local conditions. Concerns that are well known — either within a region or throughout the nation — and whose borrowings involve large sums obtain most of their credit in a broader market, either regional or nationwide. Such business concerns can and do adjust their demand for loan funds, region by region, in response to changing conditions in financial markets.

In such ways local markets are linked into regional markets and in turn into a broad national market, with interest rates in various regions kept in fairly close alignment. If lendable funds are scarce and costly in one center, the local supply will tend to be augmented by an inflow from centers where funds are more abundant and cost less, or the demand for funds will shift to centers where the supply of funds is larger. As a result, well established borrowers — small as well as large — with a high credit rating can obtain loans from banks or other lenders on much the same conditions in one city as in another. There are many regional credit centers, but a large share of the nation's credit and money market business is transacted in or through New York City.

Market for U.S. Government Securities

The national credit market tends to pivot on the market for U.S. Government securities, which cuts across money and capital markets. If both new financing and refunding are included, the U.S. Treasury is the largest single borrower in the credit market.

Treasury securities furnish a default-free outlet for short- and long-term investments; they are actively traded; and all of them — especially the short-term issues — are an efficient medium for making marginal portfolio adjustments, such as shifts into or out of cash as needs for working funds by businesses and institutions change. In view of the character of the instrument, Treasury obligations are widely held by institutional and other investors, and their yields have a strong influence on investor decisions in other markets.

Size. At the end of 1962, Treasury debt outstanding amounted to approximately $300 billion. Of this total about $200 billion was in the form of marketable issues, that is, issues that may be bought or sold in the market prior to maturity. For the year 1962 as a whole the volume of trading in marketable issues — including transactions among dealers — amounted to well over $400 billion. Most of this amount, about 80 per cent, occurred in issues that were due within one year. As the time to maturity lengthened, the volume of trading became smaller. And the volume in the long end of the market, where issues maturing in, say, more than ten years are traded, accounted for only about 2 per cent of the total.

The short end of the U.S. Government securities market is very active for a number of reasons. Foremost is the fact that commercial banks — as well as other financial institu-

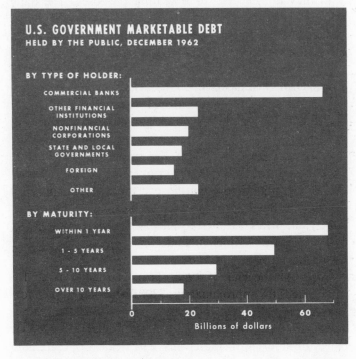

NOTE.—Based on data from Treasury Survey of Ownership, and also on Federal Reserve estimates.

tions, such as savings banks, insurance companies, and savings and loan associations — invest a large part of their operating or secondary reserves in short-term Government securities. Also, many businesses, State and local

89

governments, and foreign governments invest in such securities any excess cash or funds being accumulated for large payments or kept as contingency reserves. In general, the short-term end of the Government securities market provides an interest-earning lodgement for liquid funds until they are needed for operating purposes. The daily sales and purchases by thousands of institutional investors and businesses make for a steady stream of trading in these securities.

Commercial banks also hold substantial amounts of longer-term U.S. Government securities, especially securities maturing in from one to ten years. Other financial institutions too invest in such obligations and also in very long-term issues.

Activity. Practically all of the trading in marketable Treasury securities is conducted over the counter instead of on an organized security exchange. About twenty primary dealers in Treasury obligations handle most of it, largely on orders executed by telephone or telegraph. Most of these dealers, which include six large money market banks, have their main trading offices in New York City.

Government security dealers carry a sizable inventory of securities, and they generally buy for or sell out of their own accounts. Orders come into them directly from large customers or are channeled to them through commercial banks or stock brokerage firms. The dealers operate in a very competitive market and stand ready to quote bid and asked prices for very sizable blocks of securities. Typical transactions in Treasury bills are carried out in blocks of $1 million or more, whereas trading in long-term bonds tends to be in somewhat smaller units. Odd-lot transactions involving a few thousand dollars of securities are generally handled by commercial banks as a customer service. These banks may carry small trading positions for this purpose, or they may go through the primary dealers to execute the transaction.

Services. The Government securities market performs a very useful and important service for investors. Under normal circumstances, even the largest institutions can make portfolio adjustments at current market prices and can secure rapid execution of their orders. This is particularly true of transactions in shorter-term Treasury securities. Transactions in longer-term securities too can usually be consummated with a minimum of delay and price adjustment. However, discontinuities — stemming from the inability of buyers and sellers to agree on terms within a reasonably short period of time — are more prevalent in the market for long-term issues, especially if very large amounts are involved.

Because of its size, its continuing activity, and the default-free nature of obligations traded, the market for U.S. Government securities is highly sensitive to changes in general credit conditions. For all these reasons, it provides a touchstone by which to assess prices and yields in other parts of the credit market. Moreover, since the U.S. Government securities market is the focal point for supply and demand pressures in the money and capital markets, interest rate movements in this market are a help to the Federal Reserve in its task of evaluating general credit developments.

The market does more than indicate developments, however. It conveys the impact of the Treasury's financing programs and of Federal Reserve monetary policy to the credit market generally. The first impact of monetary policy is generally on the Government securities market because these are the securities that the Federal Reserve purchases and sells in the open market, as the next chapter describes, and because it is for the most part in these securities that commercial banks make portfolio adjustments as their reserve positions change.

All these functions of the market are most effectively performed if the market is free to register the changing choices and expectations of its many business, institutional, and individual participants, whether they be buyers or sellers. With active and continuing participation by diverse economic groups, the market can reflect, in the financial area, the economy's choices in the use of resources over time; it can provide a basis for rational calculation of credit conditions by the business and financial community; and it can readily accommodate Treasury and Federal Reserve financial and monetary activities.

Market Role of Economic Groups

In the over-all credit market no one group plays a single market role — that is, as lender only or as borrower only — although an individual group may tend to be more one than another. For example, groups that are primarily savers, such as individuals or consumers, are also ultimate borrowers. Similarly, groups that are primarily borrowers, such as businesses, also advance funds to markets. The net position of each group in relation to the credit market reflects both supplier and user roles. While the net position of any one group varies with the course and pattern of economic activity, some groups have consistent and typical roles.

Consumers as a group generally advance more funds to

the market than they borrow; most of their funds are advanced through financial institutions as intermediaries. Businesses, on the other hand, generally raise more funds than they advance. Thus, funds flow in large part from consumers to financial institutions to businesses.

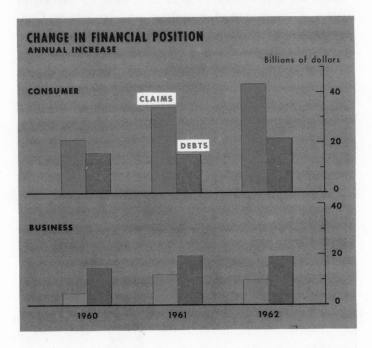

Like businesses, State and local governments in the aggregate generally borrow more funds than they advance. The Federal Government's role fluctuates with its budgetary position; it is a net source of funds when tax and other receipts exceed cash outlays and a net borrower when outlays are running ahead of receipts. Foreign transactors, too, lend and borrow in our credit market; the importance of these borrowers increased in the latter part of the 1950's and during the early 1960's.

Supply of Credit

Ultimately, the main source of funds to the credit market is the saving of consumers and businesses. Consumers save more than any other sector of the economy, as shown in the chart, and their saving makes up the bulk of funds coming into the market.

Consumers. During the past decade consumers have on the average provided about three-fifths of the economy's gross saving. Gross saving of consumers is the amount of current income not spent for current consumption on

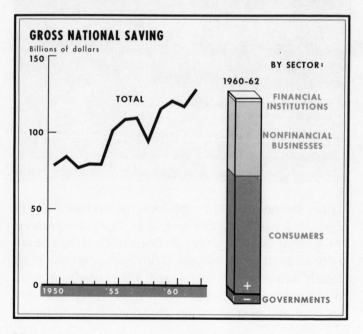

GROSS NATIONAL SAVING
Billions of dollars

TOTAL

1960-62

BY SECTOR:

FINANCIAL INSTITUTIONS

NONFINANCIAL BUSINESSES

CONSUMERS

+

−

GOVERNMENTS

such items as food and clothing. Part of such saving goes directly for purchases of consumer capital goods — automobiles, other durable goods, and homes; part flows into financial assets; and part is used to repay debts incurred earlier. Of course consumers — like other groups in the economy — may finance their purchases of capital goods or their acquisitions of financial assets by incurring new debt or by drawing upon existing holdings of assets. The amount that consumers save and the portion going into the credit market are affected by many factors, such as incomes, interest rates, capital values, and forward expectations.

When consumers acquire financial assets or repay debt, they make funds available to the credit market. When they purchase bonds, stocks, and other credit instruments, they supply funds directly. When they put their saving in savings deposits, saving and loan shares, premiums on insurance policies, and contributions toward pensions, their funds still flow into the market — not directly, but through savings institutions as intermediaries. Consumers may also use some of their saving to increase their checking account balances at commercial banks.

Since the end of World War II there has been a comparatively rapid expansion of financial institutions engaging in an intermediary function. Consumer saving that flows into these institutions reaches ultimate borrowers when the financial institutions advance funds by buying market instruments such as corporate or government bonds, real estate mortgages, and short- or intermediate-term paper of varying negotiability.

During the first three years of the 1960's the amount of consumer saving reaching the credit market indirectly through financial institutions averaged $31 billion a year. In contrast, the amount flowing directly from consumers into credit market instruments averaged only about $2 billion, as shown in the following table. In earlier years, when interest rates available from financial institutions were lower relative to market rates, a somewhat higher proportion of consumer funds flowed directly into credit market instruments.

Businesses. Businesses in the aggregate are primarily borrowers rather than lenders in the credit market, but at the same time they regularly generate a large flow of internal saving in the form of retained earnings and depreciation allowances. They use the largest part of this internal saving to finance replacement of capital goods or to expand working and fixed capital. Nevertheless, they do make some funds available to the credit market.

Business investment in financial assets is in large part temporary, however. When businesses plan to expand, they often accumulate internally generated funds for a period, and they hold these funds in some liquid asset pending their expenditure for plant and equipment. Or they may have liabilities accruing over time — as, for example, taxes — and accumulate holdings of liquid assets in anticipation of a large payment on some particular date. Sometimes — if market conditions are favorable — they borrow funds ahead of projected capital expansion and invest the proceeds in highly marketable short-term paper. Ordinarily, businesses keep the amounts in their demand deposit accounts close to the minimum needed for working purposes, but when market rates of interest on prime short-term paper are low, they may keep more of their liquid funds in these accounts.

Supply of and Demand for Funds, 1960–62

(Annual averages, in billions of dollars)

Instrument and sector	Amount
Supply quantities	
Flows into financial assets, total [1]	**100.9**
Credit market instruments [2]	*51.8*
Consumers	2.3
Nonfinancial businesses	.2
Financial institutions	42.4
Governments	5.7
Rest-of-world	1.2
Fixed-value claims on financial institutions [3]	*35.8*
Consumers	31.3
Others	4.5
Other assets [4]	13.2
Demand quantities	
Incurrence of debt and other liabilities, total [1]	**96.7**
Credit market instruments [2]	*51.0*
Consumers	18.0
Nonfinancial business	18.0
Financial institutions	4.1
Governments	8.5
Rest-of-world	2.4
Fixed-value obligations of financial institutions [3]	35.6
Other liabilities [4]	10.1

[1] Net flows. For example, purchases of credit market instruments are net of sales, and increases in debt represent extensions net of repayments.

[2] Consists of Federal, State, and local government securities, corporate bonds and stocks, mortgages, consumer credit, and bank and other loans.

[3] Consists of currency and demand deposits, savings deposits and shares, and saving through private life insurance and pension funds. Excludes funds raised in credit markets by financial institutions.

[4] Consists of security credit, trade credit, proprietors' net investment in noncorporate business, saving through government life insurance and pension funds, and miscellaneous items.

NOTE.—Federal Reserve flow-of-funds data. Differences between supply and demand quantities (including paired subtotals) reflect statistical discrepancies. Details may not add to totals because of rounding.

Businesses also supply credit directly to their customers, either individuals or other businesses. Such credit may represent a use of funds generated by the activity of the particular business, or it may represent funds borrowed from such sources as banks, other businesses, or even the capital market.

Governments. Like businesses, governmental units are usually net borrowers as a group, but they do supply funds to markets, often for special purposes. A large part of the funds advanced by governments, however, particularly those out of retirement funds, represent the reinvestment of a net inflow of saving from consumers. Such funds are usually invested in long-term obligations.

Special governmental programs affect the volume of funds in specific markets. This is illustrated by home mortgage programs of the Federal Government. The Government provides funds when a Federal agency purchases mortgages from lenders in the secondary market. Such operations enable lenders to make additional mortgage credit available.

Repayment of debt by governments supplies funds to credit markets. When governments repay obligations held by market institutions, funds become available to those institutions for relending. Funds repaid to individuals and nonfinancial business may also enter the credit market. If the individuals use such funds to finance expenditures that would otherwise have been financed by borrowing, the repayments affect credit markets through a reduction in individual demands for credit.

Savings institutions. Savings institutions advance funds to credit markets mainly by relending or investing the current saving of others. The availability of new saving to particular types of financial institutions reflects on the one hand the aggregate flow of income, the level of interest rates, and other factors that affect the amount of saving in financial form in the economy and on the other hand the preferences of individuals, businesses, and governments for different types of financial assets. Some funds flow into financial institutions under contractual arrangements such as insurance contracts and retirement funds, and the flow of such funds is little affected by economic fluctuations or variations in interest rates.

Savings institutions also make funds available to credit markets from their retained earnings, from capital stock issues, and from borrowings, but these are all relatively small sources of funds for them.

Commercial banks. The amount that commercial banks may lend depends on the availability to them of reserve funds. The amount of reserves in turn is influenced by the credit and monetary policy of the Federal Reserve System. But the amount of commercial bank lending is also influenced by the extent to which the public chooses to place its savings funds in the banks' time and savings accounts. Banks are required to hold smaller reserves against these accounts than against their demand deposits. Hence for any given total of reserves, the larger the proportion of a bank's time deposits, the more credit the bank can extend. In providing reserves to member banks, the Federal Reserve must take into account the growth rates of the two types of deposits.

Credit Supplies from Financial Intermediaries

In the aggregate, financial institutions advance directly to the credit market more funds than any other sector in the economy. These funds are advanced mostly by banks and other institutions that obtain deposits or deposit-type claims from individuals and others and invest the funds in market instruments. These investments take the form of bonds, real estate mortgages, stocks, and other loans.

The different types of intermediary institutions, however, participate in differing degrees in the short-term and long-term sectors of the market. To an important extent, these institutions are influenced in the kinds of loans and investments they make by the nature and source of their funds — that is to say, by the character of their liabilities. Legal restrictions and administrative regulations may also affect the kind of lending and investing activity.

Commercial banks have the shortest-term liabilities of all financial institutions. At the end of 1962, demand deposits made up about three-fifths of their liabilities to depositors, and time and savings deposits two-fifths. Bank capital amounted to less than 10 per cent on average of their total resources. Because demand deposits show wide seasonal or other temporary variations, banks must be prepared to meet large drains on their deposits and consequently on their reserves.

For this reason banks in general tend to lend on short- or intermediate-term maturities, although they do make some long-term loans. At the longer end of their lending are real estate mortgage loans. Instalment loans to businesses may also be of fairly long maturity. But most lending — including loans to businesses, consumers, brokers and dealers, and nonbank financial institutions — is under comparatively short-term arrangements.

The security portfolio of a commercial bank is also weighted in the direction of shorter- and medium-term

100

instruments. These are for the most part issues of Federal or other governmental units. Commercial banks have also stressed investments in longer-term securities in periods when their time and savings deposits have grown rapidly in importance.

Liabilities of mutual savings banks and of savings and loan associations are savings deposits and savings shares, held mainly by individuals. The rates of withdrawal from such accounts are much lower than those from checking accounts and somewhat lower than from savings and time deposit accounts at commercial banks. Consequently these institutions hold longer-term assets to a greater extent than commercial banks. They invest principally in mortgages and hold any liquid funds mainly in U.S. Government obligations. Mutual savings banks also invest moderate amounts in other marketable securities.

The obligations of life insurance companies to their policy holders and of pension plans to their participants are largely long-term and relatively predictable in character. These institutions, accordingly, invest most of the funds they receive in long-term capital market instruments.

All of these intermediary financial institutions add breadth and flexibility to the credit market. As a result of their development, individuals can hold liquid assets such as savings and loan shares or can safeguard the future through life insurance policies and pension plans, and at the same time ultimate borrowers can have access to a wide range of sources for short- and long-term credit.

Demand in the Credit Market

Variations in the amount and composition of credit demand have an influence on the supply of funds in the

101

market because businesses, individuals, and financial institutions have the flexibility, within limits, to alter both the aggregate amount and the kinds of credit they make available. As lenders, they respond to changes in the level and structure of interest rates, which are influenced in part by emerging credit demands from the various sectors of the economy.

On balance, consumers and businesses borrow the largest amounts from the market. In the first three years of the 1960's, each of these two groups raised an average of about $18 billion a year through the medium of credit market instruments. Governments — Federal and State and local combined — borrowed an average of $9 billion a year, and financial institutions $4 billion.

Consumers obtain funds chiefly through long-term home mortgages and short- and intermediate-term consumer credit instruments. They use short- and intermediate-term loans to finance outlays not only for such durable goods as autos and household equipment, but also for household repairs, education, and travel and for meeting personal emergencies of various kinds. They may obtain such credit from banks, sales and other finance companies, and credit unions, or from retail stores.

Mortgage debt of consumers originates primarily in connection with their purchases of homes. Like all forms of debt, however, it may also finance other expenditures. Or it may enable the borrower to retain financial assets that he might otherwise have had to dispose of, or even to add to such assets.

Nonfinancial businesses raise funds in the capital market — mainly to help finance expansion of plant and equipment — by issuing bonds, preferred and common stocks, and mortgages. Those that need funds to carry inventories or to meet other short-term requirements rely heavily on bank loans with short- and intermediate-term maturities. Borrowing for these purposes is often under a line of credit. Such an arrangement enables a regular business borrower to obtain funds up to a certain amount for short periods of time without further negotiation. Some businesses also raise short-term funds through sales in the open market of their own commercial paper or of bankers' acceptances, which bear the endorsement of a bank. Businesses sometimes borrow at banks for longer-term capital expenditure programs as well as for short-term needs.

Governments raise funds mainly by issuing securities. The specific kinds of marketable securities issued by the U.S. Government include Treasury bills, which are sold on a discount basis and have maturities up to a year; certificates, usually having maturities of one year; notes, with maturities of one to five years; and bonds, with maturities of more than five years. The U.S. Government also issues nonmarketable securities, of which the principal types are savings bonds sold to the public and special issues to Government trust funds.

State and local governments issue mainly long-term bonds, but they also borrow on short-term securities or loans and tax-anticipation notes. State and local government obligations are distinguished by the fact that interest received from them is exempt from Federal income taxes.

There are a number of specialized financial institutions that obtain almost all of their funds from the credit market. These include sales and consumer finance companies, mortgage companies, and security dealers, which borrow heavily from banks. Such institutions, in turn,

103

make credit available to their customers, so that on balance their role as lender tends to offset their role as borrower insofar as the net impact on the credit market is concerned. But because they are active on both sides of the credit market, they are distinguished from intermediary financial institutions such as banks and savings and loan associations, which obtain only a relatively small amount of their lendable funds in the credit market.

Competitive Relationships in the Market

Demand and supply pressures in the credit market tend to arise from the activities of particular sectors of the economy — consumers, businesses, and governments — and may first be focused on a part of the credit market. Enlarged borrowing by businesses or consumers tends to be reflected in developments in the particular markets most closely related to their changing financial needs, such as markets for long-term securities or for short- and intermediate-term credit, including bank loans.

For example, greater demand by businesses for credit may first be reflected in a rise in interest rates on corporate bonds. Or if there is an easing of market conditions because of reduced demand or increased saving by consumers, this may be reflected in lower rates or more liberal terms for instalment credit and mortgages. Because of the interrelationship of markets, however, such developments are soon felt to some degree throughout the whole credit market structure.

All borrowers compete to some degree for available funds, but competition is most apparent for similar kinds of credit. For example, U.S. Government demands for both short- and long-term funds compete directly with demands from private business for credit with similar maturities.

Competition also arises from the fact that a borrower can raise funds for a particular purpose in a variety of ways. For example, within limits a corporation has the option of raising funds through a bank loan or a bond issue. If it obtains the funds from a bank loan, the bank has less funds for financing short- and intermediate-term consumer borrowing. Similarly, if it sells a bond issue, this competes with the financing needs of governments and with the needs of consumers for mortgage funds.

More broadly, any one group of borrowers competes to some degree with all other groups of borrowers, regardless of whether such groups actually are, or have the option of, engaging in similar types of financing. This stems from the fact that the composition of funds flowing into credit markets is noticeably responsive to the changing composition of demand.

Funds supplied to markets shift among alternative uses in response to differential movements in interest rates or to changes in other conditions, such as the economic outlook, which in turn may affect interest rate movements. Nevertheless, flexibility of supply is neither immediate nor complete, in part because supplies respond to changing conditions only after a lag and in part because of legal, institutional, and other restrictions.

Markets are also linked through the ability of lenders to obtain funds in one market and make them available in another. This can be illustrated by the behavior of banks. As demand for credit expands, commercial banks may sell securities out of their investment portfolio to obtain funds to lend to, say, nonfinancial businesses. This in-

105

creased supply of securities competes with other securities coming into the market and tends to drive up interest rates in the market.

Interest rates in the securities market thus are affected by the demand for bank loans and, in turn, they have an effect on the terms and conditions on which such loans are made. As the effect of an increase in demand for bank loans spreads through credit markets in this way, it influences the terms on which the Government can obtain new funds in the securities market.

With sectors of the credit market closely related and with enlargement in the size and scope of the market, partly because of the growth of financial intermediaries, sources of credit available to borrowers have become extensive, competition on the side of supply has become more intense, and the potentiality for accelerated credit expansion has increased. The emerging patterns of supplies and demands in credit markets provide important information that helps the Federal Reserve in its efforts to adapt credit and monetary policies to the current situation.

Because market sectors are related in the ways described, the effect of reserve banking policy on bank reserve positions, and hence on the possibilities for expansion in commercial bank credit and in money, is transmitted throughout the national credit market. Monetary policy, therefore, has an influence on borrowing and lending throughout the entire economy.

CHAPTER VI

INTEREST RATES. *Interest rates are the prices paid for borrowed money. They are established in credit markets as supplies of and demands for loanable funds seek balance. Movements of interest rates are influenced by the nation's saving and investment, by market expectations, and by the flow of bank credit and money.*

INTEREST rates are the prices paid for use of credit. The instruments of monetary policy have an influence on the economy in part through their impact on these prices. But in a market economy many factors go into the formulation of interest rates. They are established in the credit market by the interplay of the many forces of demand and supply, including the impact on credit supply associated with the use of monetary policy instruments. The pricing function of interest rates is to bring the supply of and demand for funds into balance. In this process interest rates influence the volume and composition of available loan funds and their allocation among competing economic activities.

Variations in interest rates exert incentive and disin-

107

centive effects on individual seekers and suppliers of funds. These effects derive directly from the pricing role of interest rates and indirectly from their role as capitalization rates by means of which future streams of income may be translated into present-day capital values.

This chapter describes briefly the relationship of contract (coupon) rates to market interest rates, considers fluctuations in the interest yields on different types of loans and investments, discusses the underlying economic processes that affect interest rate formation, and describes how actions of the banking system influence movements in interest rates.

Contract Interest Rates and Market Yields

Most obligations traded in the market bear a specified contractual rate of interest to maturity. This rate is stated ordinarily in interest coupons attached to a bond and hence is known as the coupon rate. The coupon rate is to be distinguished, however, from the market rate of interest or yield to maturity, which is the rate as of today that the market is prepared to pay or accept in exchanging present for future purchasing power.

The extent to which the market rate departs from the coupon rate depends on the changing demand for an obligation in relation to its supply. As demand rises relative to supply, the market price of an obligation rises and the market yield declines because market participants pay a higher price to obtain the same fixed interest return. The opposite occurs when demand falls relative to supply; market interest rates then rise as a lower price is established in the market for the same interest income.

The amount of variation in market price that is associated with a divergence between market yield and coupon rate is affected by the length of time an obligation has to run until it matures. As an example, assume that an obligation with a coupon rate of 2½ per cent per annum and a current market rate of 3½ per cent per annum will mature in only six months. A market price of about 99½ for the obligation would make the coupon rate, the market rate, and the maturity consistent with each other.

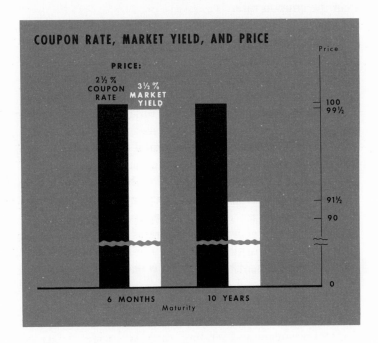

If, as a contrast, we assume a ten-year maturity on an obligation of similar coupon rate and similar market rate, then the market price would be 91½. The current market price for the longer-term security has to be lower than that

109

of the short-term obligation in order to provide the investor with an equal percentage return, that is, for the two maturities to be equally attractive from the standpoint of yield. That is to say, for the long-term issue to yield an average of 3½ per cent over the ten-year period, the current market price must be low enough that the gain in capital value over the period, together with annual payments, will make the market yield 1 per cent higher than the coupon rate.

Some short-term negotiable securities, notably Treasury bills and bankers' acceptances, do not have a contractual rate of interest specified for the investor. The yield on a new issue is determined entirely by the discount from par at which the obligation is sold. Its subsequent market price depends, as with coupon bonds, on the yield at which market participants engage in transactions and on the effect on this yield of changes in period to maturity.

When we speak of fluctuations in market rates of interest, we usually refer to changes in the yields at which existing obligations are traded in the market. We assume that new borrowers in the market will have to pay at least this rate. In general, coupon rates and actual market yields on new securities will be a little higher than this as a special inducement to investors to make purchases.

Differences Among Interest Rates

Reflecting the many purposes and situations that give rise to borrowing and lending, there is a wide variety of loans and investments in credit markets, each bearing an interest rate. Some interest rates are relatively high, and some relatively low. The particular level for each security reflects the distinctive characteristics of the obligation, the particular class of borrowers using it, and the preferences that lenders and investors may show for it.

Observable differences in market interest rates are affected by a wide variety of factors. Among the most important are the maturity structure of market instruments, that is, whether short- or long-term; the market's evaluation of differences in factors related to risk, including the business experience of borrowers and the kinds of

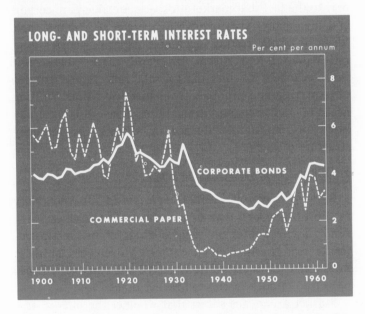

LONG- AND SHORT-TERM INTEREST RATES

Per cent per annum

CORPORATE BONDS

COMMERCIAL PAPER

assets or guarantees that back up their obligations; whether the loan is large, readily negotiable in form, and often traded in the market, or whether it is relatively small, less negotiable, and seldom traded; tax exemption features; and the varying supplies that lenders make available in given circumstances for different uses.

111

During the postwar period interest rates on securities having a short maturity have generally been below long-term rates, but this was not always true in earlier periods. There have been prolonged periods when short-term rates were above long-term rates. In addition, the relationship between the two has varied with business cycles.

In general, tendencies for short-term securities to bear lower interest rates than other obligations are related in part to the fact that market prospects are always uncertain and that many types of investors prefer to commit their funds in prime, readily negotiable paper of shorter term rather than in longer-term, less readily marketable securities. The extent to which market rates reflect these features of term, risk, and negotiability changes over time. Shifting needs of borrowers and evaluations of investors naturally exert an important influence in altering the maturity structure of rates.

How Interest Rates Move Over Time

Both borrowers and lenders have considerable flexibility in substituting one type of instrument for another. As a result, interest rates on various kinds of market instruments tend to fluctuate together. Movements in these rates differ, however, in both degree and timing. This has been true in both recent and earlier times.

Market experience shows that whether the interest rate of a particular instrument responds continuously to a changing market situation — that is, rises or falls by small increments from day to day, or even from hour to hour — depends on the character of the instrument as well as on the nature of market demand and supply. Interest rates on obligations designed for and traded in central credit and security markets respond quite sensitively to changes in either demand or supply.

Some interest rates, however, respond only slowly to shifting market conditions. Examples include rates on smaller business loans, on consumer loans, and on mortgage loans.

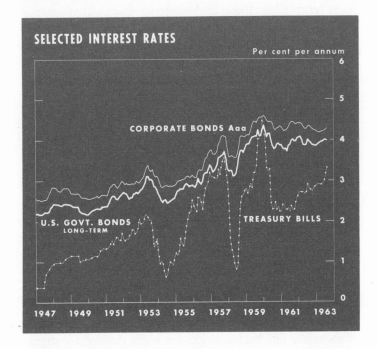

For still another group, rates are adjusted administratively in steps as conditions warrant. Examples include the rate charged by commercial banks to prime customers, the rate charged member banks by Federal Reserve Banks, and rates paid bank customers on their savings and time deposits. These rates are influenced by institutional, administrative, or legal factors in addition to the interplay of market supply and demand forces.

Changes in credit conditions accompanying changes in business activity are felt in both short- and long-term markets as a rule. Rates in these markets generally rise and fall together, but fluctuations are normally greater in short-term rates than in long-term rates. There are a number of reasons for this.

For one, movements in short-term interest rates reflect to a considerable extent the shifting ease or tightness of bank reserve positions. As described earlier, banks often make their initial asset adjustments to changing reserve availability by buying or selling short-term securities of prime quality.

In addition, fluctuations in short-term rates reflect the highly variable expectations of investors about their cash positions and needs for liquidity and about the near-term economic and credit situation. These movements in rates are influenced especially by the shifting attitudes toward liquidity of large investors, such as business corporations and financial institutions. These investors, in managing their changing requirements for funds, tend to look upon short-term paper as an interest-earning store of value that is a close substitute for non-interest-earning cash. Hence, they sell or buy short-term paper when their cash funds temporarily fall below or exceed levels desired for trans-actions needs.

The less extreme fluctuations in long-term interest rates, as compared with short-term rates, reflect in part the tendency for owners of long-term securities to regard such issues as investments that they expect to retain for extended periods. Therefore, any decisions they make to buy, sell, or hold such securities are based for the most part on longer-run economic prospects. Under these circumstances, near-term and temporary factors influence the market demand for and supply of long-term securities much less than they do shorter-term obligations.

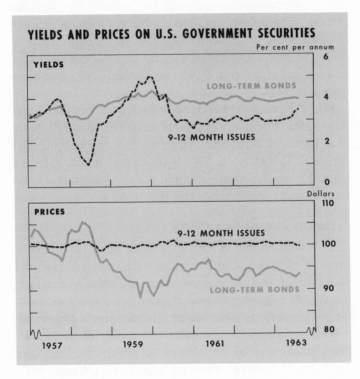

YIELDS AND PRICES ON U.S. GOVERNMENT SECURITIES

Market yields on longer-term securities reflect evaluations of market conditions that may prevail in the more distant future as well as current and near-term market conditions. Estimates of yields for the near-term will necessarily be more variable than for more distant years, in part because possible instabilities in the more distant future cannot be projected with any confidence, and in part because cyclical movements in credit conditions tend to even out over a span of years. The greater stability of yield estimates for the more distant future will counteract the greater variability of yield projections for the near future. Accordingly, long-term interest yields, which are in some sense weighted averages of yields expected over both the short- and longer-run future, will usually show smaller upswings and downswings than will short-term rates.

While short-term interest rates fluctuate more than long-term rates, prices of long-term securities fluctuate more than prices of short-term securities for reasons indicated earlier in this chapter. This is illustrated in the chart on page 115, which shows yields and prices of short- and long-term Government securities in recent years.

Factors in Interest Rate Changes

Variations in the supply of and demand for loanable funds of enough strength to change the level and maturity structure of market interest rates are usually the joint product of a number of underlying economic forces. Insofar as the maturity structure of interest rates is concerned, it is influenced by the comparative liquidity of credit market instruments; by the degree to which liabilities and functions of different financial institutions influence their preferences for short- and long-term securities; by expectations of active market participants about future rates; and by the relative supply of securities outstanding in different maturity categories.

All of these forces, which have been individually discussed in this and earlier chapters, are continuously working on the maturity composition of market interest rates. Sometimes they tend to reinforce each other, but at other times they may be offsetting.

For instance, an increase in the outstanding amount of short-term U.S. Government securities available to the nonbank public and a decrease in the outstanding amount of long-term securities would tend — if no other forces were at work — to raise short-term and lower long-term interest rates. This tendency might be reinforced by market expectations. On the other hand, offsetting changes in the market's demand for securities may well occur over time as a result of changing institutional preferences or the persistence of countervailing expectations. In a well organized and flexible credit market, dynamic adjustments are constantly under way as temporary market factors give way to more lasting influences.

In fact, because of competitive relations in the credit market, the various market interest rates generally respond together to changes in fundamental economic forces, though some rates move more readily, more rapidly, and more extensively than others. Basic influences on the central tendency shown by all rates — that is, on the average level of interest rates — include changes in the nation's saving and investment propensities, changes in market expectations as to the future course of economic activity and of prices, and changes in the flow of bank credit and money.

Saving-investment process. From a saver's point of view the rate of interest can be viewed as a price that translates present saving into future buying power. For example, at a 5 per cent annual interest rate, $100 saved from present income will exchange for $105 after a year. Meanwhile,

117

since the saver has not spent his $100 — that is, has refrained from current consumption to this extent — his saving permits resources to be used to an equivalent dollar amount for the nation's investment in plant and equipment, durable goods, and housing (or in net foreign investment).

A nation's saving represents the amount by which its members have refrained from using income to buy goods and services to be consumed currently. The investment of this saving, which represents expenditures for tangible wealth (plus or minus the net change in claims on foreigners), increases the economy's capacity to produce goods and services in the future. This increase, when realized, takes the form of added output of goods and services from which borrowers are able to pay the interest earned by the nation's saving.

Interest is, on the one hand, an earning on saving and, on the other, a cost of investment in buildings, equipment, or other capital goods. Movements of interest rates, therefore, can be said to reflect the balancing of saving and investment tendencies at given levels of output and prices. But the demand for investment in relation to the economy's willingness to save also affects a nation's real output as well as the market prices of the goods and services that have been produced. The extent of influence depends on the economic and financial organization of a country, on the phase of its economic cycle, and on specific economic conditions at the time.

In recession periods the plant facilities of a country turn out a volume of goods and services below their capacity. In these circumstances an increase in investment demand relative to the supply of saving is likely to lead to the financing of a larger volume of real investment, and thus to increased output and rising real income. The rise in real income from the expanded investment demand will generally be accompanied by an increase in saving. This will limit any tendency for interest rates to rise, and saving and investment may be brought into balance at little net advance in either interest rates or in the level of prices for goods and services.

In times of economic boom, however, when plant capacity is fully or almost fully utilized, investment demand in excess of available saving works progressively to intensify upward pressures on interest rates and price levels. Under these conditions the extent to which saving may be increased out of a rise in output and real income is necessarily limited.

Role of expectations. Shifts in expectations of businesses and consumers as to the future course of prices, production, and income affect saving, investment, and interest rates. Two kinds of effects can be distinguished. First, there are the very short-run effects, felt mainly in short-term markets and not closely related to basic tendencies in saving and investment. Second, there are the longer-term effects on saving and investment, which have a more pervasive and sustained impact on interest rates.

How shifts in business expectations may affect interest rates in the short run is illustrated by what typically happens in credit markets in the early stages of a cyclical recovery. Under these conditions interest rates — particularly short-term rates — usually rise faster than basic demand-supply developments warrant. This rise is influenced by prospects of rapid expansion in economic activity, high and rising demands for credit, and a possible shift in

119

Federal Reserve System operations from being appreciably stimulative to being less stimulative and eventually restraining.

Conversely, market expectations that the near-term economic outlook is unfavorable may precipitate a sharp decline in short-term rates. At such times prospects will loom large for a significant reduction in borrowing demands and for an increase in the supply of funds as a result of more active bank credit expansion under the stimulus of monetary policy. Interest rate movements of this short-term type may slow down markedly, or even be reversed, if it becomes evident that the market's expectations are not to be realized.

Longer-run effects of expectations may include dislocations in the saving-investment process and may thereby have more enduring effects on conditions in credit markets. For example, upward pressures on interest rates and commodity prices become and remain intensified during periods when high capacity utilization is accompanied by widely prevalent expectations of inflation. In such periods potential borrowers are stimulated to obtain immediate financing in order to beat the expected higher costs of business plant and equipment in the future. Investors also take steps to protect themselves against the expected inflation. For instance, they purchase inflation hedges such as equities and land rather than debt obligations, and they also borrow to finance these purchases.

When inflationary expectations are modified, the process is reversed. Investors' preferences for debt obligations relative to equities become stronger; yields on equities tend to rise; and upward pressures on interest rates are displaced by declining tendencies.

120

Money and bank credit. Fluctuations in market rates of interest are affected not only by changes in the saving-investment process and in the economy's expectations but also by changes in the supply of bank credit and money. When bank credit expands, banks buy securities and make loans for financing economic activity, and this adds directly to the supply of funds available. Thus interest rates may fall in response to this expansion in supply.

When bank credit expands, the supply of money typically rises. Increases in the supply of money not matched by increases in the public's desire to hold cash have one of two effects or some combination of them. As one alternative, the supply of funds in credit markets may rise further as the public attempts to substitute other financial assets for cash; if so, downward pressures on market rates of interest may be accentuated. As another, consumers and businesses may spend larger amounts on goods and services as they try to reduce the amount of cash they hold.

Interactions. The factors influencing the supply of and demand for loanable funds and the levels of interest rates — that is, the money supply, saving and investment, and expectations — are not independent of each other. The behavior of one is influenced by and impinges on the movements of the others. Changes in interest rates, output, and prices are a product of their joint effects.

When economic activity declines and investment demand falls relative to saving, interest rates tend to fall. At such times reserve banking actions to increase the availability of credit and the supply of money will make for easier credit market conditions, declining interest rates, and a financial environment and expectations favorable to a revival in economic activity.

When the economy is at a high level of capacity utilization, when demands for goods and services tend to exceed the capacity to produce them at current prices, and when investment demand is outrunning the propensity to save, prices and interest rates tend to rise. Under these circumstances reserve banking actions will generally be designed to keep credit and monetary expansion in line with the economy's growing capacity to produce and thereby to contain inflationary pressures.

Unlimited expansion of bank credit and money in these conditions, in order to satisfy all demands for credit at pre-existing interest rates, would enlarge the dollar amount of both saving and spending without relieving the shortage of real resources. It would thus result mainly in rising prices and expectations of further rises. It would not check, except perhaps temporarily, a pronounced tendency for interest rates to rise. Thus for monetary policy to be an effective influence toward stable prices and sustained economic growth, interest rates need to fluctuate in response to variations in economic activity, the supply of saving, and investment demands.

Interest Rate Inflexibilities

Some market rates of interest, as was mentioned earlier, do not reflect immediately changes in the supply of credit relative to demand but respond to such changes after a lag. In some instances a stated interest rate may not change, but the effective rate may be varied through other changes such as the amount that banks require borrowers to leave on deposit or the extent to which investors require compensation for purchasing securities having a maximum interest rate, such as Government-insured mortgages.

122

As credit demands press actively against the supply of funds in market sectors where interest rates tend to be less flexible, lenders allocate funds among borrowers on a basis other than price. Lenders, who always tend to be selective to some degree in satisfying borrowers, adhere to stricter lending standards and screen creditworthiness of borrowers more carefully when credit conditions are tight. Borrowers then become obliged to shop more intensively to find lenders whose loan standards and terms they can meet, and some borrowers fail to find accommodation.

Thus, an increase in demand for funds relative to supply not only causes interest rates to rise but also has a direct effect on the ease with which borrowers can obtain funds and the amount they can obtain. Similarly, developments that limit the supply of funds relative to demand, including those that limit bank credit expansion, are accompanied by both rising interest rates and increased nonprice allocation of funds as standards for lending become more strict.

Federal Reserve Actions and Interest Rates

Federal Reserve policy, which has its immediate impact on the availability of bank reserves, affects market interest rates in several ways. The main influence of monetary policy on interest rates is exerted by the increase or decrease in the supply of funds in the market that results from multiple expansion or contraction of bank credit based on fractional reserve requirements. On the average, however, only a small share of aggregate credit demand is satisfied through the bank credit expansion that is associated with growth in money supply. Available estimates indicate that the share so satisfied averaged about 6 per cent annually during the decade ending in 1962.

123

The Federal Reserve can initiate a change in bank reserves through its open market operations or, when appropriate and feasible, by changes in reserve requirement percentages. Federal Reserve purchases and sales of Government securities in the open market, of course, have some immediate impact on interest rates. By conducting most of its operations in short-term securities, the market for which is much broader than markets for longer issues, the System tends to minimize this immediate impact. Purchases have been made, however, in the intermediate- and long-term area in an effort to reduce even further the downward pressures on short-term rates at times when this has appeared to be desirable, such as in periods when short-term capital outflows have been intensifying a balance of payments problem.

Since open market operations in securities of either short or long maturity bring about larger changes in the supply of funds — through multiple expansion or contraction of bank credit — their basic impact is on rates in all sectors of the market, which come to be affected in some degree. Flexible adjustment between short- and longer-term interest rates is an essential aspect of a responsive credit market. Such a market continuously reflects evolving borrower and lender preferences in the commitment of financial resources into the future. Continuous market adjustments enable the nation's financial institutions to function effectively in the public interest, as they mobilize the saving of numerous individuals and others and channel the funds into investments.

The Federal Reserve discount rate is related to and interacts with interest rates in the market. As was explained earlier, the Federal Reserve discount rate is kept in close alignment with short-term interest rates in order to avoid giving member banks either too much or too little incentive for using a facility that is intended to meet banking contingencies and temporary needs for reserve funds. While the discount rate is administered in relation to the level and structure of market interest rates, market rates themselves are primarily the product of the forces of demand for and supply of credit, including of course the effect of other Federal Reserve actions affecting bank reserves.

Because of psychological factors in the market, bank credit and monetary policy may have some effect on interest rates in addition to, and even prior to, those resulting from changes in bank reserve positions. However, interest rate movements prompted by expectations of prospective reserve banking action are not likely to be long sustained unless accompanied by changes in basic supply and demand conditions.

The course of interest rates is necessarily affected by reserve banking action, as monetary policy influences the availability of bank reserves and the flow of bank credit and money in response to developments in domestic economic activity and in the balance of payments. Reserve banking operations, however, attempt to interfere as little as possible with investor, lender, and borrower decisions as to the specific commitment of financial resources over time.

CHAPTER VII

INFLUENCE OF RESERVE BANKING ON ECONOMIC STABILITY. *Federal Reserve influence on the flow of bank credit and money affects decisions to lend, spend, and save throughout the economy. Reserve banking policy thus contributes to stable economic progress.*

E ARLIER chapters have described the mechanism of Federal Reserve influence on the flow of bank credit and money, explained the structure of credit markets, and discussed important factors affecting movements in interest rates. This chapter clarifies the relation of reserve banking measures to domestic economic stability and growth, while the next relates reserve banking to the balance of international payments.

Reserve banking policy attempts to provide a financial climate conducive to sustainable growth in output, employment, and consumption under conditions of relative stability in the average level of prices and of long-run balance in our international payments. However, these objectives cannot be attained through reliance on monetary

127

policy alone. Their accomplishment also depends on fiscal and other governmental policies and on policies of private institutions and organizations.

The posture of Federal Reserve monetary policy at any moment — whether restrictive or expansive — is a reaction to prevailing economic conditions. Monetary policy functions restrictively when inflationary tendencies are present. In other circumstances it functions expansively or assumes a posture somewhere between stimulation and restraint. To help avoid the dangers of economic downturn, reserve banking works to prevent speculative or otherwise unsustainable expansion of bank credit.

The diagram on the opposite page shows in a simplified way how actions taken by the Federal Reserve System influence total spending and thereby contribute to the ultimate objectives of high employment, maximum production, and stable prices.

The Federal Reserve carries out its responsibility for the public interest by influencing the reserves of member banks. As the diagram shows, that is where the initial impact of reserve banking policy falls. As banks respond to changes in the availability of reserve funds by altering their lending and investment policies, reserve banking comes to influence the supply of money, the availability of credit, and the cost of money in various credit markets.

Some observers stress the influence of reserve banking in terms of its effects on the money supply, others emphasize the impact of changes in the availability and cost of credit, and still others stress its effects on over-all liquidity. In the functioning of the economy each of these modes of influence has a role, and in the discussion that follows each is taken into account.

128

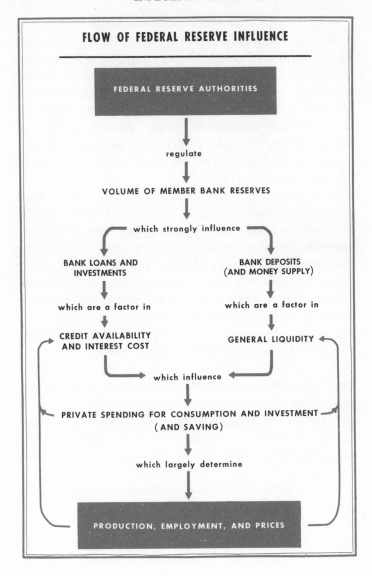

FLOW OF FEDERAL RESERVE INFLUENCE

FEDERAL RESERVE AUTHORITIES

regulate

VOLUME OF MEMBER BANK RESERVES

which strongly influence

BANK LOANS AND INVESTMENTS

BANK DEPOSITS (AND MONEY SUPPLY)

which are a factor in

which are a factor in

CREDIT AVAILABILITY AND INTEREST COST

GENERAL LIQUIDITY

which influence

PRIVATE SPENDING FOR CONSUMPTION AND INVESTMENT (AND SAVING)

which largely determine

PRODUCTION, EMPLOYMENT, AND PRICES

REACTIONS OF COMMERCIAL BANKS

What is the reaction of commercial banks to changes in the supply of reserves? For example, what is their reaction to limitations on reserves in a period of strongly expanding demand for bank loans? When they are in this situation and therefore under reserve pressure, banks are more reluctant to make new loans and interest rates on the loans they do make tend to rise, as compared with periods when their reserves are rising rapidly as the result of reserve banking policy.

In a period in which policy is limiting bank credit expansion, a bank that seeks to expand its loans rapidly may have to obtain funds by selling Government or other securities (mainly short-term) in the market, by permitting its holdings of maturing issues to run off, or by drawing down balances with, or borrowing from, other banks. Discounting at Reserve Banks, as emphasized before, is primarily for meeting passing contingencies and is not, in the U.S. banking system, a source of funds to individual banks for financing permanent loan expansion.

If a bank sells securities, lets maturing issues run off, or draws down its balance with another bank, its action will necessarily affect other banks. In the case of security sales, for example, the buyer is likely to draw down his account at another bank to make payment. Consequently, banks as a group cannot expand their total loans and investments in this way.

If many banks try to obtain additional reserves by selling securities, the amount of short-term paper or securities in the market will be increased significantly. This increased supply tends to lower prices and to raise yields on all such paper. Similar market pressures may result if banks, in order to build up their reserves, allow maturing issues to run off or draw upon balances with correspondents.

At the lower prices and higher yields, Government and other short-term securities will be more attractive. In order to buy them, nonbank investors may use temporarily idle deposits or they may even be induced to economize on cash balances held for current payments. When banks sell short-term paper to other investors and use the proceeds to make loans, ownership of deposits may shift from holders of idle balances to borrowers who are spenders and will shortly disburse the proceeds. To the extent that this occurs, the velocity of existing deposits will increase. In this process, the volume of money transactions increases as the existing supply of money is used more actively.

As banks see their short-term securities or secondary reserves declining, however, they become increasingly reluctant to reduce these securities or reserves further in order to make additional loans. This leads banks to raise interest rates on loans and to adopt more selective loan standards.

In addition, as market interest rates rise — a development that is reinforced by bank sales of securities — security prices decline and sales of securities may involve book losses. Banks are influenced to some extent by potential capital losses on the securities in their portfolios, and they hesitate to sell securities at a loss. Income tax considerations and strict earnings calculations, however, may moderate or even negate the deterrent effect of such losses on continued sales of securities.

At times when monetary policy aims at stimulating bank credit expansion to help counteract recessionary tendencies in the economy, banks will find their reserve funds increasing quite rapidly. In using these funds, they are likely first to repay any outstanding indebtedness to the Reserve Banks, particularly if loan demands are weak or declining as might be expected under the conditions assumed. After they have reduced their borrowings, banks will begin to purchase short-term securities, thereby rebuilding their secondary reserve positions and reinforcing any tendency already existing in the market toward declining interest rates. They will also begin to relax their loan policies and this, together with reduced interest rates, may actively encourage the extension of bank loans that were postponed or that were not encouraged by lenders under the earlier conditions of credit restraint.

EFFECTS OF CHANGES IN THE MONEY SUPPLY

Changes in bank reserve availability influence changes in the money supply. What is the response of the economy to changes in the rate at which the supply of money is growing, under the influence of monetary policy?

At each level of income and interest rates, there will be an amount of money that the public wishes to hold for transactions, or for precautionary or speculative purposes. Suppose that actions taken by the Federal Reserve fail to provide the desired amount of money. In that event some reaction is likely to be registered both in spending and in interest rates.

In an attempt to reestablish its desired level of balances, the public may spend less, or it may sell off financial assets (or purchase fewer of them), with a consequent rise in interest rates. As interest rates rise in this situation they too influence decisions to spend and to save. Also, the rise in interest rates affects the demand for money balances, as it leads people to accommodate themselves to smaller cash balances.

On the other hand, a volume of money in excess of what the public wishes to hold leads to increased spending and lending and to reductions in interest rates.

Demand for Cash

In assessing the effect on economic activity of changes in the money supply, it is important to recognize that there is no simple automatic measure of the appropriate relationship between the amount of money outstanding and the level of economic activity. A given volume of money, for example, can be associated with either higher or lower levels of total spending — that is, can finance more or fewer transactions — depending on how often it is used. The rate of turnover, or velocity, of money indicates how much work each unit of money does in financing transactions.

Cash balances are held by private sectors of the economy for a variety of reasons. A large part of their total represents working balances, that is, amounts of demand deposits and currency held for financing regular transactions. The size of such balances varies in part with the time lag between receipts and expenditures. For example, the time that elapses between pay dates is one factor affecting the size of cash balances. People who are paid every week have smaller cash balances, on the average, than those who are paid monthly. The size of the cash balance also varies with income. The higher a person's income and expenditures, the larger his cash balance for transactions is likely to be.

Cash balances are held for other reasons too. They may

represent saving out of income, as a store of value for pre-cautionary reasons — to gain flexibility in choice and timing of purchases, to provide against a rainy day, or to antici-pate future expenditures or investments. In other instances they may be held as a store of value for speculative reasons, with the expectation of buying in case of a sharp decline in security, real estate, or commodity prices.

The size of the cash balances that businesses and indi-viduals find it desirable to hold depends in part on the level of interest rates. When interest rates are low, the holder sacrifices relatively little in holding cash rather than an asset that earns interest. The higher the level of interest rates, the greater the sacrifice in holding idle cash instead of an interest-bearing financial asset. The form in which contingency or speculative balances are held — whether it be in demand deposits that bear no interest or in interest-earning assets — is highly sensitive to the rate of interest paid.

Several types of assets are close substitutes for cash in its store-of-value function, as explained in Chapter I. These include savings and time deposits at commercial banks, deposits at mutual savings banks, shares in sav-ings and loan associations, and U.S. Government savings bonds. Short-term market instruments, especially obliga-tions of the U.S. Government, such as Treasury bills, are also close substitutes for cash because they are generally convertible into cash with relatively small risk of capital loss. Such assets possess high, though varying, degrees of liquidity. A backlog of these "near money" assets, to-gether with some holdings of cash, gives the individual consumer or enterprise greater discretion in making its decisions to spend.

Use of Cash in Relation to Monetary Policy

Changing attitudes of people toward their cash balances and liquid asset holdings get reflected in changes in the use or velocity of money. Changes in the amounts of cash and other liquid assets that individuals wish to hold are influenced by many factors. Among important influences are changes in the amount of transactions to be financed; expectations as to future levels of economic activity, interest rates, and prices; and other motives and circumstances that determine decisions to spend or save. In addition, changes in bank credit and money themselves may set in motion forces, such as changes in interest rates, that lead to changes in the turnover of money for a period of time. Changes in the public's willingness to hold cash assets, it is evident, are related broadly to movements in economic activity and, hence, are one indicator of underlying conditions making for expansion or contraction of the economy.

Efforts of reserve banking policy to curb inflationary spending by limiting expansion of the money supply are generally accompanied by more active use of cash balances by the public. Some individuals and businesses may increase their spending by drawing upon their own existing cash balances or by converting financial assets into cash. As interest rates rise in this situation, others will be induced to put their idle balances to work in interest-earning assets. Such an addition to the flow of available credit tends to offset somewhat the credit-restraining effects of anti-inflationary monetary policy.

As incomes rise in an expansionary period, however, people will feel a growing need for transactions cash, and it will become increasingly inconvenient for them to economize on existing holdings. For this reason many

135

economists believe that a rise in velocity in this situation will approach a definable limit. Another reason is that there are limits to the increases in interest rates that non-bank financial institutions can offer to induce the public to economize on cash holdings. Institutions are limited in bidding for funds because when they pay higher interest rates this affects the cost of their lending, and as lending costs rise borrowing becomes less attractive to businesses and individuals. Therefore, the ability of institutions to attract funds and to use them profitably is reduced.

When economic activity is declining, efforts to stimulate spending by encouraging expansion of the money supply may be accompanied by a less active use of cash balances. The expansionary effects of additions to bank reserves and the supply of money may be weakened, in other words, by a rise, however activated, in the public's desire to hold cash and by an accompanying decline in the velocity of money. As a result, countercyclical monetary action, even though aggressive, may not be accompanied by a commensurate rise in spending.

With the changing use of cash balances a potential countervailing force to monetary policy, it is necessarily incumbent on the monetary authorities to pay close attention to money velocity and to weigh its strength carefully in determining possible actions.

EFFECT OF CHANGES IN CREDIT CONDITIONS

Changes in interest rates and other credit conditions associated with countercyclical variations in the supply of money and credit influence economic developments through their effect on decisions to borrow and spend or to save and lend.

136

How Lenders and Savers Are Affected

Commercial banks' willingness to lend and the terms they offer are strongly influenced by monetary policy because it has a direct impact on their reserve positions. Other lenders, such as finance companies and mortgage companies, obtain part of their funds by borrowing from commercial banks. At times when credit expansion is under restraint, these lenders find that funds are less readily available and more expensive than in times of credit ease. As the volume of their borrowing is restricted and its cost rises, nonbank lenders may find it necessary to curtail their lending. They will also tend to charge customers higher rates of interest on loans.

In periods of rising interest rates, all financial institutions find that the value of their existing portfolio of assets declines, sometimes sharply. In these circumstances, particularly when the potential capital loss (after tax) is large relative to the increment to income from new loans, financial institutions are reluctant to sell assets in order to make loans.

The flow of lendable funds in the over-all credit market depends to a large extent, however, on the saving of consumers, who make funds available to the market directly or through intermediary financial institutions. Whenever the supply of saving falls short of the prevailing demand for it, interest rates rise. The rise in interest rates tends to be limited, however, by the extent to which it brings forth saving that would not otherwise have been made. Motives to save are complex, and the rate of interest return is only one of a number of incentives.

How much total consumer saving will respond in given circumstances to changes in interest rates is a matter of

137

some uncertainty. Nevertheless, changes in interest rates do have discernible effects on the distribution of the flow of consumer saving among various financial investments and also, to a degree, on the distribution of total consumer saving between financial investments and investments in capital goods.

How Borrowing and Spending Respond

The effect on borrowing and on spending of changes in credit conditions and costs will not be uniform among businesses and individuals. The effect will vary with— among other things — the reliance that is placed on credit by the potential borrower, with the borrower's financial position and credit standing, and with his income and profit expectations.

Business. In periods of restraint on the pace of monetary expansion, potential business borrowers will be discouraged in a number of ways. The pressure on banks to restrict the growth of their loan portfolios will lead them to ask some borrowers to accept smaller loans and some to accept shorter maturities. In other instances banks may ask customers to postpone their borrowing altogether. And any rise in bank lending rates may also discourage some potential borrowers from seeking loans. Customers who want to borrow are likely to seek accommodation elsewhere, but these sources — nonbank financial institutions and the credit market generally — will also be under pressure as a result of the general excess of demand at current levels of interest rates.

The net effect of receding ease and eventual tightening of credit markets is likely to be some curtailment of spending by business. Forward inventory commitments, and later the actual purchases, may be curbed; and there may also be a slowing down in planned spending for plant and equipment.

These curtailments in spending may not affect the majority of businesses or the full amount of many loans, but they will affect some borrowers and the amounts involved in some loans. In other words, marginal borrowing will be restrained. The result usually is a smaller increase in spending than transactors would have wanted under more favorable credit conditions, rather than an actual contraction in spending. For this reason, the brake on business spending is difficult to observe.

The sensitivity of business spending and borrowing to changes in interest rates and other credit terms varies widely. The ability and willingness to accumulate inventories, for example, may be significantly affected for some enterprises by a rise in bank lending rates, while for others, whose inventory costs are smaller or whose financial position is stronger, such a rise may have little deterrent impact. In certain fields such as industrial and commercial construction, public utilities, and railroads, where there are large fixed investments, long-term interest rates are a particularly significant cost factor. In such fields comparatively small increases in interest rates can result in postponement of borrowing to finance capital outlays. Even in fields where interest costs incurred for financing fixed investment may be less important, as in retail and wholesale trade, some business units may be induced to cut back on their reliance on longer-term borrowing when interest rates rise, and other borrowers may be deterred from adding to such debt. The more long-term rates rise under conditions that seem temporary, the more long-term

139

borrowers tend to postpone investment outlays because they expect to borrow later at lower interest costs.

Businesses borrow in the expectation that the return from the use of borrowed funds will exceed interest costs by a significant margin. When the margin is large and when it is fairly well assured, moderate increases in interest rates may have little effect on the willingness of a business to borrow. But when the margin is smaller or when the return is less certain, a rise in interest rates discourages borrowers.

A rise in interest rates increases the cost of long-term borrowing and influences the utilization of productive resources through changes in the relationship between prices of existing capital assets and the cost of producing new assets. These changes direct some activity away from production of long-lived, slowly depreciating capital goods and thereby free resources for an immediate increase in output of consumer goods or of producers' equipment to make consumer goods. In the fixed capital area these changes, together with changes in the outlook for profits and risks due to the altered credit and monetary situation, shift the balance of business decisions toward holding or buying old assets, and adapting such assets to new uses, as compared with producing new ones.

The relationship between capitalized values of existing assets and costs of producing new ones is indicated on the following page. The illustration pertains to an office building with a net income from rent of $100,000 a year.

If the current interest rate for such investment, with allowance for risk, were 6 per cent, the capitalized value of the existing property would be more than the cost of constructing a new building with the same earning prospects. An investor in this type of real estate would build a new structure instead of buying an existing building, other things being equal.

Estimated cost of constructing a new building..........................	$1,500,000
Capitalized market value of an existing building with earnings from rent (net of all current costs and depreciation) of $100,000:	
If current interest rate, with allowance for risk, is 6 per cent.......	1,666,667
If current interest rate, with allowance for risk, is 7 per cent.......	1,428,571

On the other hand, if the relevant interest rate were 7 per cent, it would not pay to build a new structure and the decision would go the other way. The economic resources that would have gone into constructing the new building would then be available for other uses.

Consumer. Consumers make use of both short- and long-term credit. They use short- and intermediate-term credit to finance purchases of durable goods, home improvements, and a variety of services. Most of their long-term borrowing takes the form of residential mortgages.

Various types of institutions extend short- and intermediate-term credit to consumers on fairly standardized terms and charge rates that are relatively inflexible and high in relation to open market rates of interest. The interest rate that a consumer financing institution pays for the funds it borrows is only one of the cost elements in the finance charge to consumers, but it does have an influence on the institution's willingness to lend.

General credit tightness or ease will be transmitted to

141

consumer credit through changes in the strictness or leniency of credit standards applied by institutions granting such credit. The variation of credit standards affects the volume of new credit extended, and this in turn affects the volume of consumer credit that is outstanding.

Even though the mortgage market is less highly organized than are markets for government and corporate obligations, and interest rates on mortgages are less sensitive to shifts in supply or demand pressures than are rates on other securities, the financing available for home purchases is considerably affected by credit conditions and interest rates.

Some lending institutions increase or decrease sharply the proportion of lendable funds they are willing to place in mortgages when interest rates on competing investment media fall or rise significantly. This tendency may be especially pronounced for Government-underwritten mortgages — FHA-insured or VA-guaranteed — because administrative ceilings on their contract rates make their actual market rates less flexible than those on other media.

As the availability of residential mortgage funds fluctuates, potential borrowers may encounter more or less difficulty in qualifying for mortgage loans. Borrowing to buy houses is typically long-term and repayable in monthly instalments. The ability of a potential borrower to qualify for a mortgage usually depends on the relationship of the monthly payment to his income. The standards that lenders apply in this respect depend in large measure on the availability of mortgage funds, and these standards become more stringent as the amount of funds available for lending declines.

In addition, any increase in interest rates on mortgages

adds to the monthly payment. Thus marginal borrowers are no longer able to qualify on the basis of existing loan standards regarding the relation of the monthly mortgage payment to monthly income. In periods when over-all demand for goods and services is tending to be excessive, limitations on the pace of monetary expansion and on the availability of credit, together with increases in interest costs, tend to discourage house building or to encourage preferences for lower priced houses. In periods of economic slack and credit ease, increases in loanable funds and lower interest rates encourage residential construction.

TIME SEQUENCE OF EFFECTS ON SPENDING

The effect on the economy of changes in the flow of bank credit and money work themselves out over time. For example, when productive resources are intensively utilized, limitations on bank credit expansion will generally mean that income payments to individuals do not increase as they might have. This restraint on income will be gradual and will be accompanied by abatement of the pressure of demand against the supply of goods.

Both consumers and businesses will spend less, and the spending of each group will influence the spending of the other. That is, curtailed spending for consumer goods and other finished products will have a dampening effect on producers' demands for machinery and other equipment required to make such goods, while curtailed business spending in its turn will restrain consumer income and spending. Consumers and investors may anticipate these secondary effects and, through their attitudes and actions, may bring them about more promptly and in greater degree.

143

In a period of inflationary pressures such developments work to restore stability in the economy. In this process, any increased tendency to restrain spending and correspondingly to enlarge the flow of financial saving out of current income helps to correct forces making for inflationary tendencies. This enables a larger proportion of borrowing demands to be met out of increased financial saving, which reduces pressures leading to expansion of bank credit and money.

On the other hand, in a period when the total demand for goods and services tends to be slack in relation to current output, the stimulation to spending that arises from easier credit conditions will be multiplied over time. Increased activity arising from credit ease will add to the volume of money income available for subsequent spending, thereby expanding the demands of consumers for goods and services and strengthening business incentives to improve and add to production facilities.

As the flows of spending, investing, and saving in the economy change in response to monetary policy and also to other circumstances, the reserve banking authorities are in a position to adapt current policies to these developments. If spending is tending to react too strongly or too weakly to policy shifts, the stance of policy can be altered. The gradualness with which policy has its effect, together with the inherent flexibility of monetary instruments, enables the reserve banking authorities to adapt to changing circumstances. At the same time, policy needs to be sensitive to, and also to anticipate, current economic tendencies and what they are likely to mean for the near-term future. Through these efforts the timing of policy is made consonant with the evolving course of the economy.

144

Monetary Policy and Growth

This chapter has described how the economy responds to reserve banking efforts to maintain economic stability. It has dealt primarily with responses to countercyclical monetary policies — that is, with responses to a restrained expansion in bank credit and money during inflationary periods and to an encouraged expansion in recessions.

In contributing to economic stability at high levels of employment, monetary policy helps to create a favorable environment for sustainable long-term growth with a reasonably stable value for money. The rate of growth of the economy over time depends in large part on the extent to which resources are devoted to expansion of industrial plant and equipment, to agricultural improvements, to education and the development of technical skills, to research, and other similar items. Thus it hinges on the saving-investment process, described in Chapter VI.

The willingness and need of a country to invest for long-term growth depends on a whole complex of economic, social, and political elements. Among important factors are the rate of technological innovation, the need to use existing technology to catch up with more advanced countries, and a country's growth and development over the years. For instance, a country such as the United States, which has grown rapidly in the past, is more in a position to use its existing resources to produce consumption goods and services than are other less advanced countries. Less advanced countries, on the other hand, need to stress investment in plant, equipment, and agriculture strongly — through use of new technology or the more intensive application of existing technology — in order to realize growth potentials.

In our free society, choice in the use of resources is made in part through public decisions as to taxation and governmental spending, but it depends for the most part on decisions of a multitude of individuals and businesses expressed in competitive bidding in the market for goods,

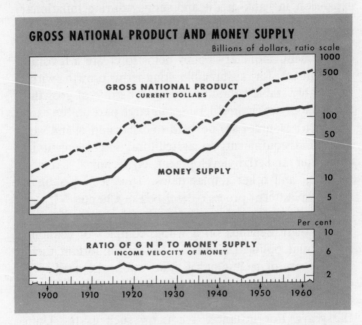

services, and the financial assets that serve as a medium for savings. Efforts by the reserve banking authorities to minimize cyclical fluctuations in economic activity while encouraging relative stability in average prices and balance in our international payments help to create an environment in which the economy will be able to grow at a pace consistent with the aspirations and energies of the people.

Still, it is clear that bank credit and money need to

expand sufficiently over the longer run to facilitate whatever rate of economic growth is consistent with the way the public wants to allocate economic resources between production for present and production for future consumption, at high levels of employment and with reasonable stability in the average level of prices. The appropriate rate of expansion in bank credit and money will be influenced by the share of bank credit in total credit and by changing habits of the public with respect to the kinds of assets in which they hold liquidity. Thus, while monetary authorities adapt their policies to continuing short-run changes in economic conditions, they must also keep in mind the public's long-run needs for cash balances.

CHAPTER VIII

THE BALANCE OF PAYMENTS. *Our economy is part of the world economy. Prices and interest rates here interact with prices and interest rates abroad, and the interrelationships affect our international balance of payments. In its decisions on monetary policy the Federal Reserve has to take the U.S. balance of payments into account. Operations by the System in foreign exchange markets help to cushion unusual supply or demand pressures in these markets.*

THE presentation in preceding chapters has been deliberately simplified by keeping to a minimum all discussion of international economic relationships. This chapter shows how these relationships affect the balance of payments between the United States and the rest of the world, and it explains why and how Federal Reserve policy is modified to help deal with international payments problems. When the aims of monetary policy are broadened to include exerting some influence on the balance of payments, decisions about policy become much more complicated.

With one exception, the actions of the Federal Reserve that can influence the balance of payments are, broadly speaking, no different from the actions it takes to influence domestic monetary conditions. The exception, the one special type of action that is taken in relation to external affairs only, is intervention in the foreign exchange markets. The concluding section of this chapter discusses the foreign exchange operations of the System.

What Is the Balance of Payments?

The term "balance of payments" is used in two main senses. It sometimes refers to the whole complex of international business and financial transactions involving payments between one country and the rest of the world. In its other sense the term refers to the *difference* between receipts and payments resulting from certain transactions — such as in goods, services, and long-term capital — between one country and other countries during some specified period; in this second sense the term is often abbreviated to simply the "balance."

When people speak of the balance on current account, they mean the surplus (excess of receipts over payments) or the deficit (excess of payments over receipts) resulting from all current transactions. By the phrase current transactions they mean all sales and purchases of goods and services, together with gifts and grants.

Examples of current transactions that give rise to receipts by the United States from the rest of the world are U.S. exports of goods, foreigners' expenditures for travel in the United States, payments of dividends and interest by foreigners to U.S. residents, and so forth. Similarly, various sorts of current transactions give rise to payments from the United States to the rest of the world. Special mention may be made here of Government grants. In many instances there are no monetary payments to foreign countries in connection with these grants, but nevertheless the grants are counted as "payments" offsetting the "receipts" nominally accruing from the exports covered by grants.

But current transactions are not the only kind of international transactions. There are also capital transactions. Examples of these are loans, investments, changes in holdings of bank deposits, and shifts in the ownership of gold reserves.

Because there are different ways in which international transactions of these two broad kinds can be classified, terms such as balance, surplus, and deficit have different meanings depending on the particular classification being employed.

For many purposes of analysis the most useful and important classification is one that combines all current transactions and many capital transactions that relate to nonliquid assets — particularly, but not exclusively, long-term investments and loans. In such a classification, the resulting surplus (or deficit) is equal to the increase (or decrease) in the country's net liquid asset position in relation to the rest of the world.

From an international point of view, a country's liquid assets include its gold reserves and in addition, depending on the precise details of the classification being used, various other official and private assets abroad. Against these liquid assets there are various liabilities, which may also be viewed as foreigners' liquid assets held in this country. This type of classification is used in the official

U.S. balance of payments statistics, which are compiled and published by the Department of Commerce.

These statistics help to show the causes of gold movements between the United States and other countries and to explain changes in foreign holdings of liquid assets in the United States, such as deposits in U.S. banks and investments in U.S. Treasury bills or other liquid assets.

When there is a surplus in the U.S. balance of payments accounts — that is, an excess of receipts over payments on current transactions and certain kinds of capital transactions — it is often called a "favorable" balance for the United States, because it adds to U.S. gold reserves or other U.S. liquid assets abroad or decreases foreign liquid assets in the United States.

The terms "favorable" or "unfavorable" applied to the balance of payments in this sense do not refer to the total asset and liability position of the country in relation to the rest of the world. It is possible that the net international assets of the United States can increase in total, while the net liquid asset portion of the total decreases. For example, U.S. nonliquid assets abroad — chiefly long-term investments — may rise sharply relative to the corresponding foreign loans and investments here, but foreigners may increase their holdings of liquid assets here more than we increase our holdings of such assets abroad. Indeed, that is what has happened in recent years.

In the postwar period the U.S. balance of payments has been "unfavorable" in this limited sense, as the accompanying chart shows. The deficit in the accounts has been especially large in the years beginning with 1958. This deficit has been settled by large movements of gold from U.S. reserves to foreign countries and by large additions

152

to foreign holdings of liquid assets in the United States.
These foreign dollar assets belong mostly to commercial
banks and foreign and international monetary authorities

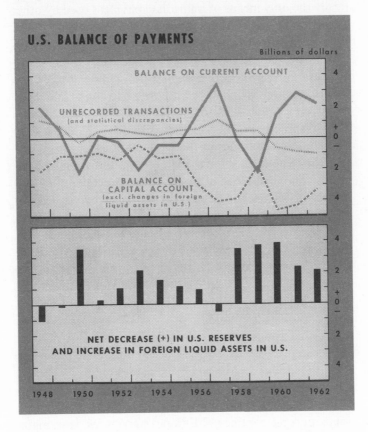

(mainly central banks and the International Monetary
Fund). But some are also held by individuals and businesses in other countries as well as by international
development lending institutions.

153

Use of the Dollar in International Payments

U.S. dollars are widely held and used by other countries for settling international transactions. And they are practically the only means of immediate payment used by other countries in their transactions with the United States. Whenever the payments from the United States to foreigners on current transactions, long-term capital transactions, and various other capital transactions exceed the corresponding payments from abroad to the residents of the United States and to the U.S. Government, there is almost sure to be, in the first instance, an increase in foreign dollar holdings in the United States.

If this amount is greater than foreign individuals, businesses, and commercial banks wish to retain, they sell dollars in the exchange markets for other currencies. To prevent the rates of exchange for their currencies from rising above specified levels — usually in accordance with the Articles of Agreement of the International Monetary Fund — foreign central banks have to buy dollars in the exchange markets. Then at their discretion, the foreign central banks may convert some part of their increased dollar holdings into gold.

Whether and to what extent a foreign monetary authority decides to let its balance of international payments affect its dollar holdings or its gold holdings depends largely on its established practice with regard to the form of its reserves. Some countries, such as the United Kingdom and some continental European countries, have made a practice of holding all of their reserves in gold except for working balances. Any substantial short-run change in their official dollar account, therefore, has been reflected promptly in purchases or sales of gold.

Some other countries have held part of their reserves in gold and part in dollars. Others have considered it advantageous to hold nearly all of their reserves in dollars. And some hold their reserves in pounds sterling, which are liabilities of the United Kingdom. When these countries convert dollars into sterling or vice versa, their operations may affect British and American gold reserves in opposite directions.

Because of the wide use of dollars both as a means of commercial payment and as a monetary reserve, variations in the dollar holdings of central banks reflect their use for settling payments balances with other foreign countries as well as payments to, and receipts from, the United States. The widespread use of the dollar as an international reserve currency makes the stability of the dollar important to other countries as well as to the United States.

Significance of the Balance of Payments

Maintaining a stable international value for the dollar is an important policy objective of the United States for both international and national reasons. If international confidence in the dollar were destroyed, the environment for sustainable long-run growth of the domestic economy would be impaired.

A healthy balance of payments is essential, in the long run, for maintaining stability of the dollar and the world's trust in its soundness. It is easy to see why this is so. Long-continued deficits in the U.S. balance of payments would put more dollars into the hands of foreign private persons and central banks than they would wish to hold. The central banks would convert these dollars into gold.

But these conversions could go on only as long as the

155

United States had enough gold to meet the demands.[1] If U.S. gold reserves were ever to become so small that substantial doubts about the ability of the United States to convert dollars into gold would arise, the dollar would cease to be an unquestioned international means of payment and reserve asset. Loss of confidence in the dollar might even be generated through a build-up of speculative fears far in advance of real dangers, if people did not see progress toward elimination of the deficit.

It is therefore important to bring about adjustments in the U.S. balance of payments. Fortunately, the possession of large gold reserves provides time for doing this in ways that will avoid disturbance of confidence. Governmental measures of various kinds can encourage an increase in exports and in other ways stimulate increases in U.S. receipts from the rest of the world and decreases in payments from this country. While these measures are gradually having their beneficial effects on the balance of payments, gold is available in ample amount to meet the demands of foreign central banks and official institutions.

Factors Influencing the Balance of Payments

The farther the world has moved from the highly restrictive framework of barriers and controls on international trade and investment that grew up in the years of the great depression and that persisted through the war and early postwar years, the more closely interrelated the economies of different countries have become. Under

[1] See Chapter IX regarding the measures that can be taken to make U.S. gold holdings available for international use in case the gold stock falls below the amount required for the gold certificate reserves of the Federal Reserve Banks.

these circumstances economic events within each of the national economies have come to be influenced more and more by events in the broader world economy.

Within the domestic economy, production and trade and borrowing and investment are guided by price and cost relationships, by profit-making possibilities, and by interest rates and credit availabilities. Exactly the same kinds of influences are at work in the broader world economy. It is true, of course, that the international influences of cost-price relationships or of differences in interest rates are less pervasive than similar influences within the domestic economy: many products and services cannot, in the nature of things, enter into international trade, and many who lend or borrow in domestic markets cannot easily shift to international markets despite the steady removal of obstacles to international capital movements. Nevertheless, international cost-price relationships, differences in profit expectations, and differences in interest rates and credit availabilities are powerful in determining the shape of a country's balance of payments with the rest of the world.

The emergence in recent years of large and continuous deficits in the U.S. balance of payments reflects in part the improved competitive position of foreign industrial countries in world trade. Large investment outlays and rapid technological advances have enabled many of these countries to offset the advantages the United States held in the early postwar years. Moreover, in 1949, the par values of many major foreign currencies were reduced, so that these currencies became cheaper in terms of the dollar. At that time these adjustments in exchange rates had little immediate impact on the balance of payments. Later, as

157

European output of exportable goods increased and controls on international trade and payments were relaxed, it became evident that the 1949 devaluations had been helpful in making European exports attractive to foreign buyers. Also, investments in Europe have become attractive to American companies.

During the period 1960 through mid-1963 the general level of wholesale prices in the United States was remarkably stable. In contrast, in many important European countries there was a rising trend of production costs and, in lesser degree, of the selling prices of goods, particularly those consumed domestically. However, international competition was intense and was a factor inhibiting price advances for internationally traded goods abroad as well as in this country.

Monetary Policy and the Balance of Payments

During most of the time since the Federal Reserve System was established, balance of payments considerations have entered little into the making of monetary policy. But beginning in 1958, there emerged a large and persistent deficit in the payments balance. In such a situation the Federal Reserve has to take closely into account the effects of monetary policy on the balance of payments.

Monetary policy affects the balance of payments in two major ways. First, it can help to improve the international competitive position of the United States through continued encouragement of domestic price stability. Therefore, the Federal Reserve aimed at avoiding so great an expansion of bank credit and money as might undermine the stability actually achieved in the average price level from 1958 to 1963. In other words, it sought to provide enough bank reserves to facilitate the financing of a growing output of goods and a fuller utilization of available productive resources while avoiding upward price pressures domestically that would reduce the trade balance and accentuate the international payments deficit.

Secondly, monetary policy affects the balance of payments because it influences capital flows between the United States and foreign countries through its effect on interest rates and credit availability. In providing reserves to the banks in sufficient volume to facilitate a strengthening of forces of domestic expansion, the Federal Reserve endeavored to do so in ways that would minimize the resultant downward pressures on short-term interest rates. Here the aim was to keep short-term interest rates as nearly as possible in a suitable alignment with short-term rates in major foreign money markets.

Experience in 1959-61 demonstrated that sizable shifts in relative levels of short-term rates here and abroad can quickly generate sizable international flows of some types of liquid funds. During 1959, relatively high rates in the United States, by attracting foreign commercial bank funds into U.S. dollar liquid assets, helped to hold down the drain on the U.S. gold stock caused by the deficit in current and long-term capital transactions. In 1960, business cycle forces here and abroad helped to improve our balance of payments on current account, but short-term capital outflows — which were partly in response to relatively high interest rates abroad — made the gold drain larger than it had been in 1959. In 1961, the outflows of those types of short-term capital that are most strongly affected by international differences in interest rates were smaller again.

In endeavoring to minimize the downward pressures on short-term interest rates associated with an expansionary monetary policy, the Federal Reserve regularly conducted part of its open market operations, beginning in 1961, in medium-term and long-term securities, as explained in Chapter III. And at times it reduced the supply of bank reserves in order to keep short-term rates firm. Without these and other actions — such as those taken by the Treasury in its management of the public debt — outflows of some sorts of liquid funds to other countries would have been larger, increasing the amount of gold sales needed to finance the deficit in the balance of payments.

Operations in the Foreign Exchange Market

Partly to help deal with problems created by the deficit in the balance of payments, the Federal Reserve System began in early 1962 to buy and sell foreign currencies in the exchange markets and in direct transactions with foreign monetary authorities. The aims laid down for its operations have included the smoothing out of abrupt changes in exchange rates and also the prevention of fluctuations in U.S. gold reserves or dollar liabilities due to temporary forces acting in the markets. In addition, two broader aims were set forth. One is to supplement the international exchange arrangements made through the International Monetary Fund. The other is to lay a basis for new solutions for the long-run problem of inadequacy of gold for meeting countries' international reserve needs.

In the nature of things, these operations cannot have any far-reaching influence on the factors ultimately responsible for the balance of payments deficit. Federal Reserve policy-makers recognized that adjustment of the balance of payments requires gradual changes in international cost-price relationships and in demand-supply relationships in international capital and credit markets. And they recognized that adjustment of the balance of payments may require a considerable period of time. Whatever contribution the Federal Reserve could make to this long-run adjustment would flow from the effects of monetary policies in influencing interest rates and credit availabilities and in helping to maintain price stability, rather than from exchange market operations.

But meanwhile, in connection with the need to sustain world confidence in the dollar, it was necessary that short-run disturbances of exchange markets by economic or political events in one country or another be kept from snowballing. With the U.S. balance of payments in deficit, it was very important to set up bulwarks against cumulative speculative movements that might start a flight from the dollar.

During 1961 the Federal Reserve Bank of New York, acting as agent for the U.S. Treasury's Exchange Stabilization Fund, had gained useful experience in operations in the foreign exchange market. This experience demonstrated that official operations in foreign currencies could help to moderate speculative movements of funds internationally. Then in February 1962 the Federal Open Market Committee decided that the Federal Reserve Bank of New York should begin to undertake foreign exchange operations on behalf of the System itself.

In actual practice Federal Reserve operations through late 1963 were of quite limited size, but arrangements had been made whereby large operations could be undertaken in case of need. The existence of these arrangements

161

was in itself a deterrent to speculative disturbances. By December 1963, reciprocal currency agreements had been negotiated with the central banks of eleven nations and with the Bank for International Settlements. By these arrangements, the Federal Reserve System put itself in a position to obtain, on call, about $2 billion of foreign currencies.

Under each arrangement, the System can obtain a stated amount of foreign currency in exchange for a corresponding amount of dollars. In the event of a drawing — which may be requested by either party — the balances acquired have to be repaid by the time agreed at the same exchange rate. This protects each party from loss should the other's currency be depreciated. The balances acquired may be invested at a pre-agreed rate of interest (the same for both parties) or they may be sold in the exchange markets or to the other party to the swap. If both parties concur, the agreements may be renewed any number of times.

The swap arrangements are available for use by foreign countries in case of need. In 1962 Canada drew U.S. dollars, under its swap arrangement with the Federal Reserve, in exchange for Canadian dollars, as part of a series of measures it took to establish confidence in the new par value of the Canadian dollar.

The Federal Reserve has used foreign currencies acquired under some other swap arrangements to buy "excess" dollars from foreign central banks that the latter had accumulated through intervention in the exchange markets. As noted earlier, for reasons of law, custom, or policy, some foreign central banks ordinarily refrain from holding more than a certain amount or proportion of their external reserves in dollars. At times when dollar accruals to the official reserves of one or another of these central banks have temporarily become very large, perhaps because of seasonal influences or perhaps because of short-run speculation, the Federal Reserve has been able to forestall temporary gold movements. In effect, foreign excess holdings of dollars are replaced — through the swap drawing and the subsequent purchase operation — by dollar assets that are protected against exchange rate risk.

The foreign currencies drawn and used under the various swap arrangements are ordinarily repaid to the foreign institution concerned within a period of months, by making use of foreign currency bought after the initial disturbance has ended. The swap arrangement is then maintained on a standby basis until a new occasion for making a drawing arises. Thus, operations under swap agreements are designed primarily as a defense against speculative capital flows and against temporarily accentuated gold drains.

CHAPTER IX

RELATION OF RESERVE BANKING TO GOLD. *Gold flows, which generally reflect balance of payments conditions, are an important influence on member bank reserves. Inflows of gold reduce the reliance of banks on Federal Reserve credit, and outflows of gold increase it. Changes in the country's monetary gold stock are reflected in Federal Reserve Bank holdings of gold certificates.*

THE previous chapter showed how the balance of payments relates to reserve banking policy. Changes in the U.S. gold stock generally reflect our balance of payments position and thus must be taken into account, along with the underlying causes of the changes, in the formulation of the over-all stance of monetary policy, whether it be stimulative, restraining, or something in between.

In addition to its special relationship to the balance of payments and its use as an international reserve, gold influences Federal Reserve policies and operations in two ways. First, reserves in gold constitute a statutory base for Reserve Bank power to create Federal Reserve credit. Second, changes in the U.S. gold stock affect the volume of member bank reserves and the use of Federal Reserve credit. This chapter explains the statutory role of gold and the technical aspects of relationships between changes in gold holdings and in the volume of member bank reserves and Federal Reserve credit.

Gold as Reserve Money

In the U.S. monetary structure the standard unit of value — the dollar — is defined by statute as a weight of gold. Gold, however, is not coined into money, and currency based dollar for dollar on gold — represented by gold certificates — does not enter into public circulation or into member bank reserves. Under the Gold Reserve Act of 1934, private persons subject to U.S. jurisdiction are not permitted to hold any gold for monetary purposes. Gold nevertheless functions as reserve money of the Federal Reserve Banks. It also functions as a means of settling international balances. These are the elements of our modified gold standard.

The Treasury is custodian of all U.S. monetary reserves held in the form of gold. Reserves of the Federal Reserve Banks take the form of certificates representing the gold, or of credits with the Treasurer of the United States payable in these gold certificates. As a technical matter, therefore, Reserve Bank holdings of gold certificates are the statutory base for its power to expand or extinguish Federal Reserve credit.

Under existing law the Reserve Banks must hold a stipulated proportion of gold certificates as reserve against their liabilities for notes and deposits, respectively. The legal minimum for the gold reserve ratio is 25 per cent for each category of liabilities. On September 30, 1963, the actual ratio was 31 per cent. This was above the statutory minimum but was down sharply from earlier levels.

When the Treasury buys gold, it pays for this gold at the established rate of $35 per fine troy ounce (exclusive of handling charges) by drawing on its deposit account at the Reserve Banks. Against the gold acquired, the Treasury credits an equivalent amount to the gold certificate account, thus providing the basis for restoring its deposit account at the Federal Reserve Banks. The new gold certificates then provide the basis for additional Federal Reserve credit.

The Treasury must hold gold at the rate of $35 an ounce for all the gold certificates that it issues or credits to the gold certificate account.[1] Consequently, while the title to the gold is in the Government, the greater part of it is held as cover for gold certificates issued to the Federal Reserve Banks or credited to their account. Only the Reserve Banks may by law own gold certificates, and these may not circulate outside the Reserve Banks.[2]

At the end of September 1963 the Treasury held $15.6 billion of gold, of which $15.3 billion was held as cover for a corresponding amount of gold certificates or gold certificate credits issued to the Federal Reserve Banks. Of the remainder, $156 million was held as a reserve against United States notes. In addition to the gold held

---

[1] The amount of gold that the Treasury must hold as cover for each dollar of gold certificates can be changed only by an Act of Congress.

[2] However, about $20 million of gold certificates issued before the Gold Reserve Act of 1934, and not turned in to the Treasury when gold and gold certificates were withdrawn from circulation, were still regarded as outstanding in the official statistics on currency in circulation at the end of 1963. But according to an Act of Congress, approved June 30, 1961, the Treasury is no longer required to hold gold as cover for the certificates that were not returned from circulation as required by law.

by the Treasury, $53 million of gold was in the working balance of the Exchange Stabilization Fund.

In addition to its responsibility as a buyer and holder of monetary gold, the Treasury sells gold to foreign mon-

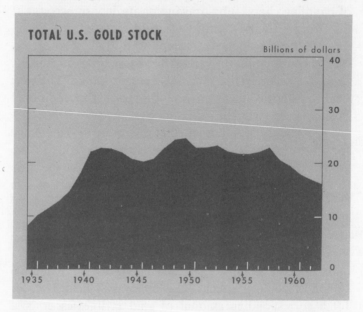

TOTAL U.S. GOLD STOCK

Billions of dollars

etary authorities for settlement of international balances or for other legitimate monetary purposes at the established price. Through these transactions foreign monetary authorities may convert their dollars into gold to increase their own gold reserves or to use in making international payments. Similarly, foreign monetary authorities can always acquire dollars, if they so desire, by selling gold to the Treasury. The Treasury conducts its gold transactions with foreign authorities through the Exchange Stabilization Fund.

Until 1961 the United States used only one method to limit fluctuations in exchange rates for the dollar in terms of other currencies to the narrow range permitted under the Articles of Agreement of the International Monetary Fund. This method was for the U.S. Treasury to buy or sell gold. Since then, however, both the Treasury and the Federal Reserve have intervened from time to time in the exchange market by buying and selling foreign currencies, as was discussed in Chapter VIII.

How Gold Is Monetized

The process by which gold produced in the United States or sold by foreign holders reaches the Treasury and is reflected in additions to the reserves of member banks and Federal Reserve Banks is described below.

The gold is taken to a U.S. assay office or to a U.S. mint. If the seller is a domestic producer, the Treasury pays for the gold by check. The seller will deposit this check with his bank, usually a member bank, which in turn deposits it with a Reserve Bank, where the amount of the check is added to the member bank's reserve balance and charged to the account of the Treasury. The Treasury will replenish its account by crediting an equivalent amount to the System's gold certificate account, and this is credited to the appropriate Reserve Bank. Assume that the gold is worth $10 million. Then the gold stock of the Treasury, the gold certificate account of the Reserve Bank, the reserve balance of the member bank, and the bank deposit of the seller of the gold will each increase by $10 million.

For many years movements of gold into and out of this country's monetary reserves have reflected almost exclusively transactions with foreign central banks, govern-

169

ments, and international institutions. When a foreign official authority sells gold, the payment is made on the books of the Federal Reserve Bank of New York by transfer from the account of the Treasury to the account of the foreign authority, and there is no immediate increase in member bank reserve balances and deposits. Such increases will occur, however, when the foreign official authority draws on its deposit account at the New York Bank to provide funds for goods and services bought in American markets, to invest in money market assets, or to transfer funds to commercial banks for other reasons.[3] The ownership of the newly gained gold certificate reserves becomes distributed among the Reserve Banks as a result of these various transactions.

On the other hand, when a foreign monetary authority wants to acquire, say, $10 million of gold, it instructs the Federal Reserve Bank of New York to charge that amount to its deposit account and to pay the Treasury. Acting as fiscal agent of the Treasury, the Reserve Bank then obtains the gold from the assay office for transfer to the foreign authority. In payment for the gold the Reserve Bank withdraws the equivalent amount from its gold certificate fund and charges the account of the Treasury for the gold certificate credits surrendered. As a result of these transactions, the gold certificate account of the Reserve Bank and the gold holdings of the Treasury each decline by $10 million.

Prior to actual purchase of the gold, the foreign authority usually increases its account with the Reserve Bank by

---

[3] Foreign deposits with Federal Reserve Banks are relatively small and generally kept at a minimum needed for working purposes. Most of the deposits of foreigners are at commercial banks.

transferring the needed amount from the market, either from existing deposits with member banks, generally acquired through its own exchange market operations, or from funds acquired through the sale of Treasury bills or other investments it had been holding. In either case both the deposits of member banks and their reserve balances will be reduced by an equal amount.

For use in balancing their international accounts, foreign central banks and governments hold large amounts of dollar assets in various forms, mainly short-term U.S. Government securities. As already indicated, they hold relatively small demand deposits with the Federal Reserve Bank of New York.

Gold transactions with foreign countries take place regularly without a physical movement of gold into or out of this country. A foreign monetary authority may purchase gold from the United States and have it "earmarked," or segregated, for its account at the Federal Reserve Bank of New York. Under such an arrangement the gold is physically held in that Reserve Bank. Conversely, a foreign authority may sell some of its earmarked gold to the U.S. Treasury.

Earmarked gold belongs to foreign authorities. It is not a part of the U.S. monetary gold stock. Foreign purchases of gold to go into, and sales of gold to come out of, earmarked accounts have the same effect on our banking system as foreign purchases of gold for export and foreign sales of newly imported gold. Transactions involving earmarked accounts are spoken of as gold movements.

The process of monetizing gold described above is essentially the same as when the Reserve Banks actually held gold. The only difference is that the title to the gold

171

owned by the United States is in the Treasury and that the Reserve Banks hold claims on it in the form of gold certificates or a credit in the gold certificate account on the books of the Treasury. The altered procedure has not changed in any significant respect the ultimate effects of gold flows on the reserves of Reserve Banks and member banks and on bank credit and the total money supply.

Gold and Federal Reserve Operations

It has been shown that gold purchases or sales by the United States increase or decrease the reserves of Reserve Banks. It has also been shown that, disregarding transitory lead-and-lag effects associated with the use by foreign official authorities of deposit accounts at Reserve Banks, gold purchases or sales by the Treasury affect the reserve position of member banks and hence their ability to make loans and investments and expand their deposits.

The ultimate effect on member bank reserves of gold movements is thus the same as that of Federal Reserve open market or discount operations. When gold flows in, it increases member bank reserves in the same way as would an equivalent amount of open market purchases or discounts by the Reserve Banks; when gold flows out, it reduces member bank reserves in the same way as would the repayment of a discount by a member bank or the sale of a security by a Reserve Bank. This is why demand for Reserve Bank credit tends to diminish when gold comes in and to increase when gold goes out.

Sometimes the Federal Reserve makes loans on gold to foreign central banks. When the proceeds of such loans are disbursed, this has the same effect on credit conditions in this country as any other advance by a Reserve Bank.

172

Federal Reserve operations can be used to offset the effect of gold flows on member bank reserves. But if the Federal Reserve cushion of "free" gold certificate holdings — that is, the excess of gold certificates over the statutory minimum required as reserves against note and

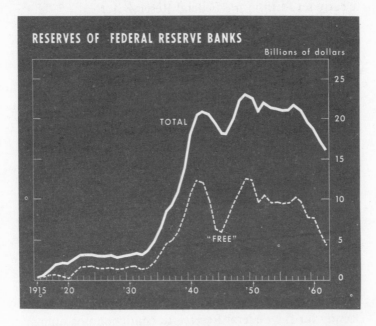

RESERVES OF FEDERAL RESERVE BANKS

deposit liabilities of the Federal Reserve Banks—were to approach and then fall below the statutory minimum, to what extent would this interfere with a stabilizing reserve banking policy? During most of its existence, as the accompanying chart shows, the Federal Reserve System has had a sizable margin of "free" gold reserves, and the reserve ratio has been in excess of the required ratio. Thus, when expansion of Federal Reserve credit has been

173

needed, it has ordinarily not been hampered by a gold reserve limitation. Nevertheless, questions about the relation between the gold reserve requirement and reserve banking policy are often asked, especially in periods of decline in the U.S. gold stock, even though the answer is clearly set forth in the Federal Reserve Act.

In effect the Act states that, if the ratio were to fall below the statutory minimum, the Board of Governors would have authority to suspend the reserve requirements, initially for a period not exceeding thirty days and then on renewal for successive periods not exceeding fifteen days. In suspending the requirements, the Board of Governors must impose on the Reserve Banks a tax that varies with the amount of the deficiencies. The tax could be nominal as long as the deficiencies were confined to reserves against deposits and the first 5 percentage points of deficiency in the reserve against Federal Reserve notes. For larger deficiencies, in the reserves against notes, the tax would have to be increased rather steeply. Moreover, the tax imposed because of deficiencies in reserves against notes would have to be added to discount rates charged by the Reserve Banks.

While the foregoing authority would provide adequate leeway for the Federal Reserve to continue to be unhampered by reserve limitations in its pursuit of policies directed to orderly economic progress, the possibility that such limitations might arise has in the past been a source of public concern. For example, the decline in the Reserve Banks' ratio of reserves to combined note and deposit liabilities during World War II threatened the Federal Reserve's freedom of policy action. In this situation the Congress in 1945 deemed it wise to reduce the reserve requirements of the Reserve Banks from 40 per cent for Federal Reserve notes and 35 per cent for deposits to 25 per cent for each kind of liability.

It should be pointed out here that as long as reserve requirements against deposits at member banks are above the statutory minima, the Federal Reserve System may increase the margin of "free" gold certificates by lowering these requirements. As member bank reserves declined in consequence of such a lowering of requirements, the amount of gold certificates that the Federal Reserve Banks would be required to hold as reserves would be automatically reduced.

Unless offset by Federal Reserve action, changes in the nation's gold reserve position have a direct bearing on the supply of bank credit. In deciding on particular actions to carry out its policies, the Federal Reserve takes into account the effect of gold flows on member bank reserves.

CHAPTER X

RELATION OF RESERVE BANKING TO CURRENCY.
The Federal Reserve System is responsible for providing an elastic supply of currency. In this function it pays out currency in response to the public's demand and absorbs redundant currency.

A N important purpose of the Federal Reserve Act was to provide an elastic supply of currency — one that would expand and contract in accordance with the needs of the public. Until 1914 the currency consisted principally of notes issued by the Treasury that were secured by gold or silver and of national bank notes secured by specified kinds of U.S. Government obligations, along with gold and silver coin. These forms of currency were so limited in amount that additional paper money could not easily be supplied when the nation's business needed it. As a result, currency would become hard to get and at times command a premium. Currency shortages, together with other related developments, caused several financial crises or panics, such as the crisis of 1907.

One of the tasks of the Federal Reserve System is to

prevent such crises by providing a kind of currency that responds in volume to the needs of the country. The Federal Reserve note is such a currency.

The currency mechanism provided under the Federal Reserve Act has worked satisfactorily: currency moves into and out of circulation automatically in response to an increase or decrease in the public demand. The Treasury, the Federal Reserve Banks, and the thousands of local banks throughout the country form a system that distributes currency promptly wherever it is needed and retires surplus currency when the public demand subsides.

How Federal Reserve Notes Are Paid Out

Federal Reserve notes are paid out by a Federal Reserve Bank to a member bank on request, and the amount so paid out is charged to the member bank's reserve account. Any Federal Reserve Bank, in turn, can obtain the needed notes from its Federal Reserve Agent, a representative of the Board of Governors of the Federal Reserve System, who is located at the Federal Reserve Bank and has custody of its unissued notes.

The Reserve Bank obtaining notes must pledge with the Federal Reserve Agent an amount of collateral at least equal to the amount of notes issued. This collateral may consist of gold certificates, U.S. Government securities, and eligible short-term paper discounted or purchased by the Reserve Bank. The amount of notes that may be issued is subject to an outside limit in that a Reserve Bank must have gold certificate reserves of not less than 25 per cent of its Federal Reserve notes in circulation (and also of its deposit liabilities). Gold certificates pledged as collateral with the Federal Reserve Agent and gold certificates deposited by the Reserve Bank with the Treasury of the United States as a redemption fund for Federal Reserve notes both are counted as a reserve against notes.

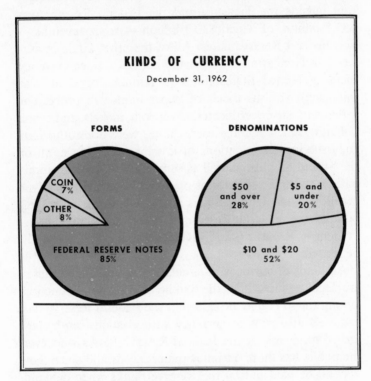

KINDS OF CURRENCY

December 31, 1962

FORMS

DENOMINATIONS

COIN 7%

OTHER 8%

FEDERAL RESERVE NOTES 85%

$50 and over 28%

$5 and under 20%

$10 and $20 52%

As our monetary system works, currency in circulation increases when the public satisfies its larger needs by withdrawing cash from banks. When these needs decline and member banks receive excess currency from their depositors, the banks redeposit it with the Federal Reserve Banks, where they receive credit in their reserve accounts. The Reserve Banks can then return excess notes

179

to the Federal Reserve Agents and redeem the assets they had pledged as collateral for the notes.

As of mid-1963 the total amount of currency in circulation outside the Treasury and the Federal Reserve was $35.5 billion, of which $30.3 billion — or six-sevenths — was Federal Reserve notes. All of the other kinds of currency in circulation are Treasury currency. Such currency includes United States notes (a remnant of Civil War financing), various issues of paper money in process of retirement, silver certificates, silver coin, nickels, and cents.

Until 1963, Federal Reserve notes were not authorized for issue in denominations of less than $5. Hence, all of the $1 and $2 bills, as well as some bills of larger denominations, were in other forms of paper money, chiefly silver certificates and United States notes. A law passed in 1963 permits the Federal Reserve to issue notes in denominations as low as $1, and silver certificates will eventually be retired.

All kinds of currency in circulation in the United States are legal tender, and the public makes no distinction among them. It may be said that the Federal Reserve has endowed all forms of currency with elasticity since they are all receivable at the Federal Reserve Banks whenever the public has more currency than it needs and since they may all be paid out by the Reserve Banks when demand for currency increases. In the subsequent discussion reference will be made to the total of currency in circulation rather than to any particular kind.

Demand for Currency

It has already been stated that the amount of currency in circulation changes in response to changes in the public's needs for pocket cash as against checking-account balances at banks. These changes are substantial and frequent. The demand varies for different days of the week, for different days of the month, and for different seasons. In agricultural regions the need for currency is heavy at

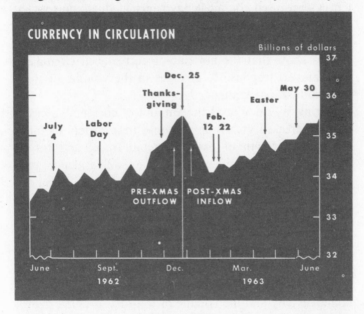

times when crops are being harvested. Throughout the country the need increases before holidays such as Independence Day, Labor Day, and Thanksgiving, when many people take trips and need more pocket cash. There is an extraordinary increase before Christmas, when cash is used for Christmas shopping and as gifts. After the holidays excess currency is deposited in the banks by the merchants, hotel keepers, and others with whom it has been spent, and the banks in turn send it to the Reserve Banks.

181

In addition to seasonal changes in the demand for currency, there are changes that reflect variations in business conditions. When business activity is rising, the need for currency to make payments increases, and when business activity declines, the need for currency also declines. Checks are used for most payments in this country, but many payments are made in currency, especially those in connection with retail trade and payrolls. Statistical studies show that the amount of currency in circulation fluctuates in response to changes in the volume of these two kinds of payments.

During World War II the amount of currency in circulation increased greatly in response to a variety of influences: the growth of payrolls, retail trade, and travel; many and widespread changes in places of residence; payments to members of the armed forces; larger incomes of people not in the habit of using banks; and no doubt hoarding of currency for various reasons. The demand for additional currency subsided after the war, but during the war in Korea in the early 1950's, it strengthened again. Over the ensuing years the amount of currency and coin in circulation has continued to expand gradually as economic activity and the volume of transactions have grown and as coin-operated machines have come into widespread use.

Effect of Note Circulation on Banking System

From the point of view of the Federal Reserve and member banks, changes in currency in circulation have a special significance that arises out of the system of reserve requirements. As has been explained, reserve requirements are expressed as percentages of bank deposits. If someone

182

borrows, say, $1,000 from a bank and leaves it on deposit to be transferred from bank to bank by check, the amount of reserves that the banking system must hold increases by only a fraction of this amount — for example, $200 if reserve requirements are assumed to be 20 per cent. If,

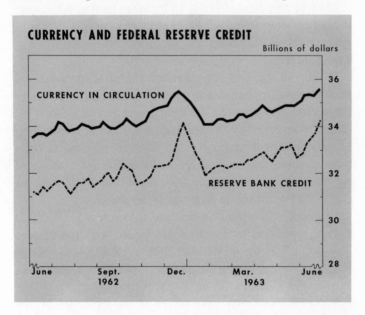

CURRENCY AND FEDERAL RESERVE CREDIT

on the other hand, the borrower withdraws the proceeds of the loan in currency, the reserves of the bank — as well as those of the banking system as a whole — decline by the full $1,000.

If the banking system had no excess reserves, it would have to obtain additional reserves whether the loan were left on deposit or were withdrawn as currency. The additional amount of reserves needed, however, would differ. The increase would be only $200 in the case of the demand for $1,000 of checking deposits, while it would be $1,000 in the case of demand for an equal amount of currency. The Federal Reserve could supply the required reserves needed by the banks by buying Government securities in the open market, if this were considered desirable, or it could lend the needed funds to member banks. Whichever procedure were followed, Federal Reserve credit — that is, Reserve Bank holdings of discounts and securities — would increase.

When the demand for currency abates, currency flows back to member banks and their reserves increase. Under these circumstances the Federal Reserve can absorb redundant reserves by selling U.S. Government securities. In general, the Federal Reserve System adjusts its open market operations so that the outflow and return flow of currency may take place with minimum tightening or easing effects on the general credit situation.

Changes in the public's demand for currency affect not only the reserves of member banks but also the reserve position of Federal Reserve Banks. When the public elects to hold money in the form of currency rather than as demand deposits at banks, this ties up more of the Reserve Banks' own reserves. For example, when the public's demand is for $1,000 in currency, the Federal Reserve Banks pay out that amount of Federal Reserve notes — and their reserve requirements increase by $250 (25 per cent of $1,000). If, however, the public's demand is for $1,000 in checking deposits, member bank reserves, which are the deposits against which the Reserve Banks must hold reserves, are required to increase by only $200, and the reserves needed by the Reserve Banks increase by only $50 (25 per cent of $200). Under the circumstances assumed, an increase in currency would tie up five times as much of the Reserve Banks' reserves as would an identical increase in bank deposits.

While the Federal Reserve pays out currency in response to the demand of the public and absorbs any currency the public does not need, it should not be concluded that the volume of currency in circulation is free of influence by the Federal Reserve. The policies pursued by the Federal Reserve affect the total volume of money in the economy — that is, the amount of currency in circulation plus the amount of checking deposits. Thus, in providing the economy with an elastic currency, the Federal Reserve must endeavor to see that the two forms of money together are appropriately related to the volume of production and trade. This means that their combined total should be neither so large as to foster an excessive demand for goods nor so small as to cause a deficiency in aggregate demand.

CHAPTER XI

BALANCE SHEET OF THE FEDERAL RESERVE BANKS.
Federal Reserve functions are reflected in the consolidated balance sheet of the Reserve Banks, known as the weekly condition statement. This statement shows how much Federal Reserve credit is being used and the key items that account for its use.

MAJOR reserve banking functions are reflected in the consolidated balance sheet of the twelve Federal Reserve Banks. The balance sheet, one of the most complete statements of its kind, is released every Thursday and shows the condition of the Reserve Banks at the end of the preceding day. The statement, known generally as the weekly condition statement, appears in the Friday issue of the principal daily newspapers of the country and is usually accompanied by explanatory comment.

The condition statement of the Federal Reserve Banks is necessarily complex because its purpose is to provide an accounting summary of all phases of Federal Reserve operations and to show, in some detail, the use of Federal Reserve credit. The nation's demand for money converges on commercial banks, especially the member banks, and through them on the Reserve Banks. Accordingly, much can be learned about current banking and financial trends by following changes in the principal items of the statement from week to week.

The balance sheet of the Federal Reserve Banks for July 3, 1963, in condensed form, is presented on the opposite page. In order to include some items that are eliminated in the consolidation process, the balance sheet used here is the combined one. The major items on it are printed in capital letters. Explanation of its items provides both a review of many important points made in earlier chapters and an opportunity to mention some technical aspects of Federal Reserve operations not heretofore dealt with.

Explanation of Asset Accounts

1. GOLD CERTIFICATE RESERVES. Although the law does not permit the Federal Reserve Banks to own gold and does not permit gold certificates to circulate, it does authorize the Treasury to issue gold certificates to the Reserve Banks. Gold certificate reserves consist of these gold certificates, of credits on the books of the Treasury payable in gold certificates, and of the redemption funds for Federal Reserve notes, which the Reserve Banks are required by law to maintain on deposit with the Treasury.

2. Federal Reserve notes of other Reserve Banks. When one Reserve Bank receives notes of another Reserve Bank, it may pay them into circulation if they are fit. If they are not fit for further circulation, it forwards them to the U.S. Treasury for retirement. This item represents notes held temporarily or in transit to Washington for retirement.

COMBINED BALANCE SHEET OF THE RESERVE BANKS
July 3, 1963

Millions
of dollars

ASSETS

1.	GOLD CERTIFICATE RESERVES............................	15,457
2.	Federal Reserve notes of other Reserve Banks...........	246
3.	Other cash...	338
4.	DISCOUNTS FOR MEMBER BANKS.........................	565
5.	Other discounts and advances..........................	..
6.	Acceptances...	44
7.	U.S. GOVERNMENT SECURITIES:	
	(a) Bought outright...............................	32,289
	(b) Held under repurchase agreement................	394
8.	CASH ITEMS IN PROCESS OF COLLECTION.................	6,779
9.	Other assets...	501
	TOTAL ASSETS................................	56,613

LIABILITIES

10.	FEDERAL RESERVE NOTES.............................	30,976
11.	DEPOSITS:	
	(a) Member bank reserves.........................	17,538
	(b) U.S. Treasurer — general account...............	884
	(c) Foreign......................................	167
	(d) Other..	192
12.	DEFERRED AVAILABILITY CASH ITEMS....................	5,257
13.	Other liabilities.......................................	77
	TOTAL LIABILITIES.............................	55,091

CAPITAL ACCOUNTS

14.	Capital paid in..	481
15.	Surplus...	934
16.	Other capital accounts.................................	107
	TOTAL LIABILITIES AND CAPITAL ACCOUNTS........	56,613
17.	THE RESERVE RATIO (per cent)........................	31.1

In a consolidated balance sheet of the Reserve Banks, this item would disappear, since the asset of one Bank is a liability of another.

3. Other cash is coin and paper money (other than gold

189

certificates and Federal Reserve notes) in the Reserve Bank vaults.

4. DISCOUNTS FOR MEMBER BANKS, an item of great interest to the money and financial markets, represent the amount of Federal Reserve credit that member banks obtain at their own initiative through borrowing and for which they have a direct repayment responsibility. Most member bank borrowings from Federal Reserve Banks, as explained in Chapter III, represent short-term advances secured by Government securities. This reflects in part the key role of U.S. Government securities among bank assets and in part the greater convenience of using them as collateral. Borrowing against Government securities or other eligible paper is done at the established discount rate; borrowing secured by other collateral satisfactory to Reserve Banks is charged a rate not less than one-half of a percentage point higher.

5. Other discounts and advances include, first, loans secured by gold made to foreign monetary authorities and, second, advances to individuals, partnerships, and corporations on the security of direct obligations of the United States. It is under the authority for this second type of advance that the Reserve Banks may lend to nonmember banks as well as other institutions against Government securities as collateral, subject to such regulations as the Board of Governors may prescribe. Rates on such loans are higher than the rates charged member banks. Loans to foreign monetary authorities secured by gold are made at the prevailing discount rate. As of July 3, 1963, no credits of either type were outstanding.

6. Acceptances are prime bankers' acceptances purchased by the Federal Reserve Banks in the open market

from acceptance dealers at prevailing interest rates. Sometimes such purchases are made under repurchase agreement whereby the seller agrees to buy them back within fifteen days or less.

7. U.S. GOVERNMENT SECURITIES comprise Treasury bills, certificates of indebtedness, Treasury notes, and Treasury bonds. Since Reserve Bank purchases of Government securities are the principal means by which the Federal Reserve can create Reserve Bank credit on its own initiative, changes in Reserve Bank holdings of these securities are watched closely by observers in the credit market. A breakdown of holdings, by type of security, is shown each week in the published statement.

Reserve Bank holdings sometimes include Government securities purchased from nonbank dealers with the agreement that dealers will repurchase them within a specified period of fifteen days or less. The Federal Reserve System makes repurchase arrangements available in periods of temporary credit stringency to help meet market needs for reserve funds and for credit when dealer inventories of Government securities are unusually large. Use of the facilities, when made available by the System, is at the initiative of the dealers. On July 3, 1963, the Reserve Banks held $394 million of Government securities under repurchase agreements with dealers.

The law authorizes the Reserve Banks to hold at any one time as much as $5 billion of Government obligations acquired directly from the Treasury. These direct borrowings by the Treasury are infrequent and of very short duration. They grow out of temporary imbalances between the inflow and outflow of Treasury funds. The Treasury draws checks for current payments on deposit accounts

191

held with the Reserve Banks. Just before tax collection dates, these accounts sometimes fall below desirable working levels. Because Treasury accounts at commercial banks through which tax payments are received may also be low at these times, the Treasury may be without adequate funds for a few days to replenish its Reserve Bank balances.

When its balances fall below working levels, the Treasury may sell special short-term certificates of indebtedness to Federal Reserve Banks to forestall a temporary overdraft in the Treasury's checking accounts. When such obligations are outstanding on the Wednesday statement date, they are reported separately in the condition statement.

8. CASH ITEMS IN PROCESS OF COLLECTION are checks and other cash items deposited with the Federal Reserve Banks and in process of collection on the date of the statement. The item has a counterpart in a technical account on the liability side of the statement, described as DEFERRED AVAILABILITY CASH ITEMS. The relationship of these two accounts yields a measure of a type of Federal Reserve credit, called "float," generated by the Reserve Banks in rendering collection services to member banks; float is further explained on page 194 under liabilities.

9. Other assets for this condensed statement consist of accrued interest and other accounts receivable, premium on securities owned, balances due from foreign central banks (including convertible foreign currencies acquired under "swap" agreements), bank premises, and various items of lesser significance.

Explanation of Liability Accounts

10. FEDERAL RESERVE NOTES, which are the principal type of currency in circulation, are liabilities of the Federal

192

Reserve Banks secured by specific collateral, as explained in Chapter X. They are a first lien on all the assets of the issuing Reserve Bank. Changes in the amount of Federal Reserve notes in circulation occur in accordance with changing demands of the public for currency and with member bank holdings of vault cash.

11. DEPOSITS consist for the most part of the reserve accounts of member banks. The aggregate of the member banks' balances in these accounts, along with their vault cash, constitutes the operating base of the banking system. The Federal Reserve influences the total flow of bank loans and investments by conducting its own operations in such a way as to regulate the volume of its deposit liabilities to member banks, while at the same time supplying to banks the amount of Federal Reserve notes needed for their own vault cash and for the public's hand-to-hand circulation.

The checking accounts of the U.S. Treasury, which it uses to make payments for Government purchases of goods and services, make up the second category of deposit liabilities. Weekly changes in the Treasury's deposit account are often fairly sizable. Although directly related on occasion to accompanying changes in other balance sheet accounts, these week-to-week changes are most often reflected in opposite changes in the reserve accounts of the member banks.

The Treasury also maintains deposit accounts with approved commercial banks for receiving taxes and the proceeds of securities sold to the public. These accounts are commonly known as tax and loan accounts. The Treasury's established practice is to maintain large enough balances in its checking accounts at the Reserve Banks to meet its current payments. It transfers funds from its commercial bank accounts into its checking accounts in accordance with its schedule of payments. Whenever the Treasury account at the Reserve Banks exceeds desired working levels, the excess may be redeposited with commercial banks. By carrying the bulk of its deposits in tax and loan accounts, the Treasury moderates the effect on bank reserves of fluctuations in its receipts and payments.

Deposits of foreign central banks and governments are the third category. These deposits are maintained with the Reserve Banks for international settlement and foreign monetary reserve purposes. Changes in the total of these deposits likewise affect member bank reserves. Such changes may also be immediately associated with changes in other accounts, particularly in gold certificate reserves, when the Treasury buys or sells gold.

Nonmember banks that pay at par checks submitted to them by Reserve Banks may keep check-clearing accounts with the Reserve Bank of their district as a matter of convenience. These accounts are part of the fourth main category, "other" deposit liabilities. Other depositors whose balances are reflected here include certain Government agencies and international organizations.

12. DEFERRED AVAILABILITY CASH ITEMS was mentioned on page 192 as the counterpart of CASH ITEMS IN PROCESS OF COLLECTION, an asset account. The former arises from the fact that Reserve Banks do not give immediate credit for all checks deposited with them for collection. The credit is deferred according to a schedule that allows time for out-of-town checks to go through the mail or by other transfer media to the banks on which they are drawn. The maximum period for credit to be

deferred is now two business days. After that, the member bank's reserve account is automatically credited.

Since the time actually taken to collect checks is often longer than that allowed in the schedules, this crediting frequently occurs before the account of the bank on which the check is drawn is debited. The difference between the asset account (cash items in process of collection) and the liability account (deferred availability cash items) represents checks that, although not yet collected by the Reserve Banks, have already been credited, in accordance with a specified time schedule, to the reserve accounts of the banks that deposited them. This difference, which is sometimes sizable, measures the amount of Federal Reserve credit or float generated by the national check collection process and available to the member banks.

13. Other liabilities consist principally of unearned discount on notes and securities, miscellaneous accounts payable, and dividends accrued between the semiannual dividend payment dates.

Explanation of Capital Accounts

14. Capital paid in. When a bank is admitted to membership in the Federal Reserve System, it is required to pay for capital stock of the Reserve Bank of its district an amount equal to 3 per cent of its own capital stock and surplus. The shares do not carry the power through voting to control the management of the Reserve Bank as does ordinary stock in private banks or corporations. The member banks are entitled by statute to a cumulative dividend of 6 per cent per annum on the paid-in value of their stock. Ownership of Reserve Bank stock may not be transferred, nor may the owning bank hypothecate its shares.

195

15. Surplus represents retained net earnings of the Reserve Banks. The Reserve Banks may draw on their surplus to meet deficits and to pay dividends in years when operations result in loss, but they may not distribute it otherwise to the stockholding member banks.

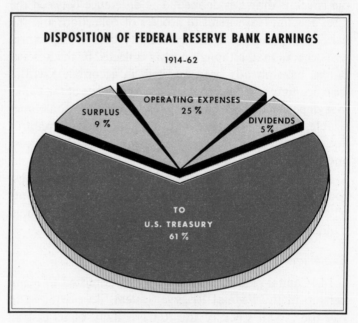

DISPOSITION OF FEDERAL RESERVE BANK EARNINGS

1914-62

SURPLUS 9%

OPERATING EXPENSES 25%

DIVIDENDS 5%

TO U.S. TREASURY 61%

While the Federal Reserve Banks earn an income, their operations are not carried on for this purpose but are determined by Federal Reserve credit and monetary policies. Over the years most of their income above amounts needed to cover expenses, including expenses of the Board of Governors in Washington and the 6 per cent statutory dividend to members, has been paid to the Treasury. Since the surplus account has come to be

196

approximately double the paid-in capital stock account, no further additions are being made to it, except when necessary to maintain this relationship with capital. The law provides that, if the Reserve Banks are dissolved, any surplus is to be paid to the U.S. Government.

16. Other capital accounts comprise unallocated net earnings for the year to the date of the statement.

The Reserve Ratio

As explained in Chapter IX, Reserve Bank holdings of gold certificates constitute their legal reserves and provide the statutory limit to the expansion of Federal Reserve credit. In recognition of the reserve function of gold, the reserve ratio of the Reserve Banks is published regularly as a memorandum item on their condition statement (item 17 in the statement on page 189).

Use of Federal Reserve Credit

The Federal Reserve Banks are not operated to make a profit, and they do not extend additional credit simply because they have enough reserves to do so. The use of Federal Reserve credit is determined principally by the policy pursued in the public interest by the Federal Reserve authorities to encourage or discourage the expansion of bank credit and money.

The degree to which Federal Reserve credit is extended depends on movements in other factors that affect commercial bank reserves and hence the ability of banks to lend or invest and expand the money supply. How the use of Federal Reserve credit varies with changes in these other factors affecting bank reserves is discussed in the next two chapters.

197

CHAPTER XII

THE BANK RESERVE EQUATION. *Federal Reserve credit, gold, and currency in circulation are the principal factors that influence the volume of member bank reserves—the basis of bank credit and the money supply. The relationship among these factors, together with other more technical ones, is sometimes called the bank reserve equation.*

MEMBER bank reserves and all of the factors that affect their volume can be combined into a bank reserve equation. In this equation, simplified in presentation on page 200, factors supplying member bank reserve funds are set opposite factors absorbing such funds. The various factors come partly from the combined balance sheet of the Federal Reserve Banks and partly from the Treasury's accounts. Together they reflect the numerous forces in the country's economic life that affect the activities of the banking system.

Over the longer run, the major factors affecting member bank reserves are Federal Reserve credit, the monetary gold stock, and currency in circulation. Other factors, which are less important in the long run, include Treasury currency; Treasury cash accounts; and nonmember bank, foreign, and other accounts at the Federal Reserve.

Any of the factors in the bank reserve equation can increase or decrease member bank reserves. On the one hand, inflows of gold, decreases in currency in circulation,

FACTORS IN THE BANK RESERVE EQUATION, MARCH 1963

(Averages of daily figures.   In billions of dollars)

Factors supplying reserve funds:

Monetary gold stock	15.9
Federal Reserve credit	32.5
Treasury currency	5.6
Total	54.0

Factors absorbing reserve funds:

Currency in circulation[1]	31.6
Treasury cash accounts	1.3
Nonmember bank, foreign, and other accounts at the Federal Reserve	1.4
Total	34.3
Member bank reserves	19.5
Total	54.0

[1] Currency in circulation outside the Treasury, Federal Reserve, and member banks. See also notes to table on p. 211.
NOTE. — Details may not add to totals because of rounding.

and increases in Federal Reserve credit add to these reserves; on the other hand, outflows of gold, increases in currency in circulation, and contraction of Federal Reserve credit decrease them. Each of these factors, and indeed other more technical ones, may be highly variable over short periods. The interaction of short-run variations is considered in the chapter that follows. This chapter discusses the longer-run interplay of the major factors in order to put the role and function of Federal Reserve credit in clear perspective.

As shown in the table, gold and Federal Reserve credit account for most of the supply of reserve funds. In addition to member bank reserves, currency in circulation accounts for most of the use of reserve funds.

The relative importance of these major factors changed from time to time over the 1934-62 period, as shown in the chart on page 203. Through 1941 the dominant factor was growth in the gold stock, whereas during the war the predominant influences were increases in currency in circulation and in Federal Reserve credit. Between 1945 and 1958, changes in these factors were smaller and more varied than in other periods. Beginning in 1958 the principal factors were an increase in Federal Reserve credit and a decrease in the gold stock.

Interplay of Bank Reserve Factors

Gold flows are greatly affected by forces outside Federal Reserve regulation. They necessarily depend on international economic, financial, and political forces as well as on forces of domestic origin. Currency movements are influenced primarily by the level of business activity and by the habits and preferences of the public for currency.

Federal Reserve credit is the balance wheel between these two more or less independent factors and member bank reserves. The extent to which the Federal Reserve System uses its credit powers depends on current Federal Reserve policy and on changes in bank reserves caused by gold or currency movements.

If the effect of gold and currency movements on bank

201

reserves is in harmony with current credit and monetary policy, Federal Reserve action to offset these movements will not be necessary. If the effect of the two independent factors is not in harmony with current policy, the System will take offsetting action. Thus, the kind of policy being pursued by the Federal Reserve — whether one of ease or one of restraint — may be associated with either increases or decreases in Federal Reserve credit, depending on the movements in other factors in the reserve equation.

Suppose the Federal Reserve is attempting to ease market conditions and to increase the reserves of commercial banks. If other factors are not adding to bank reserves, the Federal Reserve will buy Government securities, thus increasing reserve funds by the amount of the purchase. A policy of ease will then be associated with a rise in Federal Reserve credit.

Suppose, on the other hand, that large foreign sales of gold to this country and large inflows of currency to banks occur at a time of ease in current reserve banking policy. This reduces the need for Federal Reserve credit. These gold and currency movements may even be so large as to create reserve conditions that are too easy in view of domestic economic developments. Under these circumstances the Federal Reserve will temper the excessive easing of credit conditions by selling securities. A policy of ease will then be associated with some decline in Federal Reserve credit, because other factors will have contributed more than enough to an appropriate easing of member bank reserve positions.

Member bank reserves, although affected by the three other principal factors in the bank reserve equation, are not an entirely passive element. They respond to economic

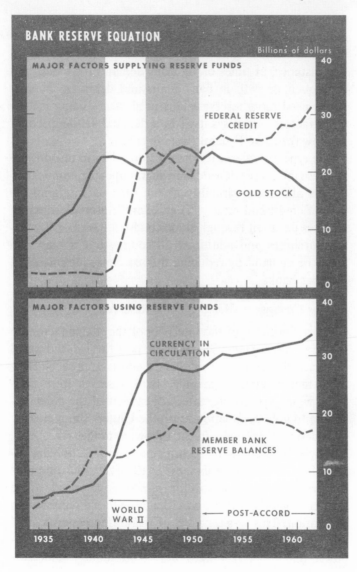

BANK RESERVE EQUATION

Billions of dollars

MAJOR FACTORS SUPPLYING RESERVE FUNDS

FEDERAL RESERVE
CREDIT

GOLD STOCK

MAJOR FACTORS USING RESERVE FUNDS

CURRENCY IN
CIRCULATION

MEMBER BANK
RESERVE BALANCES

WORLD
WAR II

POST-ACCORD

1935   1940   1945   1950   1955   1960

203

forces that are not necessarily reflected in gold or currency movements, and their independent impulses may be reflected in member bank borrowing from the Reserve Banks. For instance, at times of vigorous demand for credit and consequent growth in bank loans and deposits, member banks need more reserves. This need, if not being met by other factors, expresses itself in a demand at the discount window for more Federal Reserve credit.

The type of Federal Reserve action taken in response to all these influences depends in general upon economic conditions and the desirability at the time of enlarging the flow of credit and money. The Federal Reserve ordinarily supplies its credit through some combination of open market purchases and additional discounts, but it may also meet the demand by reducing the reserve requirements of member banks.

Prewar Changes in Member Bank Reserves

A brief account of the interplay of the major factors in the bank reserve equation over the past three decades will illustrate the usefulness of the equation approach. How these factors affected member bank reserves from mid-1934, which was shortly after adjustment of the monetary system to gold revaluation, until the United States entered World War II is shown in the following table.

It will be seen that the principal factor supplying reserve funds was a huge increase in the gold stock and that the principal factor absorbing reserve funds, aside from member bank reserves, was the growth in currency in circulation. This was a period of world depression and of unsettled political conditions abroad. As the nation's manpower and other resources were continuously underemployed, the Federal Reserve pursued a policy of monetary ease to encourage their fuller utilization. With gold inflows adding to reserve funds, this policy was effectuated with little net change in Federal Reserve credit.

MAJOR FACTORS IN BANK RESERVE EQUATION
CHANGE, JUNE 1934 – DECEMBER 1941
(Monthly averages of daily figures. In billions of dollars)

Factors supplying reserve funds:
Increase in gold stock.............................. 14.9

Factors absorbing reserve funds:
Increase in currency in circulation[1]................ 5.6
Reduction in Federal Reserve credit............... 0.1
Other factors (net).............................. 0.2
                                   ———
Total... 5.9

Increase in member bank reserves.................. 9.0
                                   ———
Total... 14.9

[1] Currency in circulation outside the Treasury and Federal Reserve. See also notes to table on p. 211.

The effect of the gold movement on member bank reserves was substantial, and excess reserves became large. And they remained large even though the Federal Reserve authorities raised the reserve requirements of member banks as economic recovery progressed. Over this entire period, banks made almost no use of Reserve Bank discount facilities.

War and Postwar Adjustment Periods

After the United States entered the war and began to provide exports under lend-lease, foreign sales of gold to this country stopped. After the war there was some further rise in gold reserves, but taking the war period and the postwar adjustment period as a whole, gold movements were a factor operating on balance to absorb member bank reserves as the following table shows.

MAJOR FACTORS IN BANK RESERVE EQUATION
CHANGE, DECEMBER 1941 – MARCH 1951

(Monthly averages of daily figures.   In billions of dollars)

Factors supplying reserve funds:
Increase in Federal Reserve credit................. 21.3
Other factors (net)............................. 2.2

Total....................................... 23.5

Factors absorbing reserve funds:
Increase in currency in circulation[1]................ 16.2
Decrease in gold stock.......................... 0.9

Total....................................... 17.1

Increase in member bank reserves................. 6.4

Total....................................... 23.5

[1] Currency in circulation outside the Treasury and Federal Reserve. See also notes to table on p. 211.

The major factors affecting member bank reserves over these abnormal years were the increases in Federal Reserve credit and in currency in circulation, most of which occurred during the war. During that period the Federal Reserve System, in support of war finance, undertook to supply enough Federal Reserve credit to enable the banking system to purchase Government security offerings not taken up by nonbank investors, to counteract the drain on member bank reserves from the increase in currency in circulation, and to support the more than doubling of commercial bank deposits. Another objective of Federal Reserve operations during the war period was to maintain a stable credit market so that Government and essential industry could obtain credit promptly and cheaply. To accomplish these purposes the Federal Reserve supplied credit freely through open market operations.

The Federal Reserve authorities carried over into the postwar period a policy of supporting prices of Government securities at close to par, thus maintaining a high degree of yield stability in this and other sectors of the credit market and continuing a policy of credit and monetary ease. In this situation Federal Reserve credit was freely available at the call of the market, and banks and other holders of Government securities were able readily to adjust their operating positions by selling these securities. Member banks had little need for borrowing at Reserve Banks.

There was a growing recognition in this period that Federal Reserve support of Government securities prices and yields at arbitrary levels was incompatible with effective Federal Reserve regulation of the volume of bank reserves. In March 1951 the Treasury and the Federal Reserve agreed on discontinuance of the policy. The major objective of the accord was to minimize the creation of reserve funds at the initiative of banks and other investors who might sell Government securities to the Federal Reserve at pegged prices and yields.

Post-Accord Period

Beginning in 1951, Federal Reserve operations were re-adapted to the flexible use of its general methods of influencing bank reserve positions in accordance with the seasonal, cyclical, and growth needs of the economy for bank credit and money. Over the next seven years, changes in Federal Reserve credit reflected a combination of open market operations, discount operations, and changes in reserve requirements. The net changes affecting bank reserve positions were relatively small, with a moderate growth of currency in circulation approximately offset by other factors, as shown in the following table. Nevertheless,

MAJOR FACTORS IN BANK RESERVE EQUATION CHANGE, MARCH 1951 – MARCH 1958

(Monthly averages of daily figures.   In billions of dollars)

Factors supplying reserve funds:

Increase in Federal Reserve credit.................	0.9
Increase in gold stock...........................	0.6
Other factors (net)..............................	1.4
Total..	2.9

Factors absorbing reserve funds:

Increase in currency in circulation[1]...............	3.4
Decrease in member bank reserves................	0.5
Total..	2.9

[1] Currency in circulation outside the Treasury and Federal Reserve. See also notes to table on p. 211.

over this period bank credit and money continued to grow as reductions in legal reserve requirements enabled banks to use existing reserves for credit expansion; as increased public preferences for time deposits, which have low reserve requirements as compared with demand deposits, also freed some existing reserves; and as banks economized somewhat further on excess reserve balances.

During this interval there were two periods of cyclical economic expansion — from mid-1952 to mid-1953 and from late 1954 to the early fall of 1957. And there were two short periods of economic recession — from mid-1953 to late 1954 and from the fall of 1957 to the spring of 1958. These cyclical movements, shown by the fluctuations in total output of factories and mines in the chart, called for changes in Federal Reserve policy.

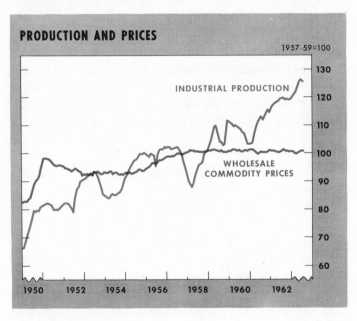

PRODUCTION AND PRICES

1957-59=100

In the expansion periods Federal Reserve policy first encouraged increases in bank credit and money; then after expansion gained momentum and inflationary tendencies developed, it restrained such increases. Restraint was effected by limiting the provision of bank reserves through open market operations. Under these circumstances, with demand for bank credit strong, member banks borrowed

209

more at the discount windows of Reserve Banks. In both the 1952–53 and 1955–57 periods their borrowings rose to more than $1 billion. While discount rates were raised only once during the 1952–53 expansion, they were raised seven times during the 1955–57 expansion — from 1½ per cent to 3½ per cent.

As expansions tapered off and during the recession periods, the Federal Reserve used open market purchases, and also reductions in reserve requirements, to provide member banks with reserves and thus to ease credit availability and stimulate expansion of bank credit. Member banks paid off much of their borrowing at Reserve Banks in the recession periods, and the Reserve Banks lowered their discount rates along with declines in market rates.

Emerging Balance of Payments Problem

During the years from 1958 to 1963, there was a substantial outflow of U.S. gold. Meanwhile currency in circulation continued to expand. These two factors absorbing reserves were counteracted by an increase in Federal Reserve credit, as the table indicates, and by the increased availability of reserves in 1959-60 when regulations were amended to permit member banks to count vault cash in meeting their reserve requirements.

In the spring of 1958 monetary policy was designed to stimulate credit expansion because the U.S. economy was in a recession. Between the summer of 1958 and the autumn of 1959, as economic recovery progressed, a policy of ease turned gradually to one of restraint. Member banks increased their borrowings from the Reserve Banks to about $1 billion, and there was a series of increases in Federal Reserve Bank discount rates.

Monetary policy in the United States came to be influenced more and more by the large and persistent deficit in the balance of payments that began in 1958 and by the objective of minimizing the related outflow of gold, as well as by the needs of the domestic economy. During and after 1960 in particular, outflows of short-term funds from the

MAJOR FACTORS IN BANK RESERVE EQUATION CHANGE, MARCH 1958 – MARCH 1963

(Monthly averages of daily figures.   In billions of dollars)

Factors supplying reserve funds:

Increase in Federal Reserve credit..................	7.9
Vault cash amendments (amounts added to reserves on effective dates)[1]..........................	2.2
Other factors (net)..............................	0.5
Total..	10.6

Factors absorbing reserve funds:

Decrease in gold stock...........................	6.6
Increase in currency in circulation[2]...............	3.2
Total..	9.8
Increase in member bank reserves.................	0.8
Total..	10.6

[1] In three stages, between November 1959 and November 1960, member banks were gradually permitted to count all of their vault cash in meeting reserve requirements.

[2] As a result of the changes described in note 1, after November 1960 the "currency in circulation" figure that affected reserves became currency outside of the Treasury and Federal Reserve Banks and currency other than vault cash held by member banks. Before November 1959, all currency outside of the Treasury and Federal Reserve Banks affected reserves. The figure here is a construct that reflects the gradual effect of the vault cash changes on the relevant currency measure.

United States to foreign countries added to the payments deficit, and monetary policy began to make efforts to keep short-term interest rates in the United States from falling so low that outflows would be further encouraged.

211

In 1960 and early 1961 there was a mild recession, but short-term interest rates did not decline so much as they had in earlier recessions. This was due in part to the mildness of the recession but also in part to official policy, which was influenced by the relation of interest rates to the balance of payments deficit. The discount rate was reduced, but only from 4 to 3 per cent. There were no changes in reserve requirements during the recession, but within this period member banks were permitted to count all their currency holdings in meeting reserve requirements.

The economy began to recover in 1961, and the expansion continued into 1963. While the volume of industrial production increased considerably, the output of the economy remained below its capacity and in mid-1963 unemployment was still substantial. In contrast with previous periods of increased output, therefore, the Federal Reserve followed a policy of monetary ease for a much longer time. Bank credit expanded rapidly; member bank borrowings from the Reserve Banks remained comparatively low; and market rates of interest showed little change as compared with other periods of cyclical expansion.

In supplying reserves for domestic economic expansion, the Federal Reserve also took account of the persistent deficit during the period in the balance of payments, which was reflected in a large gold outflow. To offset the reserve-absorbing effects of this outflow, the Federal Reserve provided some credit through market purchases of intermediate- and long-term securities, as explained in earlier chapters. This helped to minimize the downward pressures on short-term interest rates from such operations. In the fall of 1962 it also supplied reserves by reducing reserve requirements on time deposits.

Concluding Comment

The foregoing analysis indicates how the major long-run factors in the bank reserve equation are related, and how ups and downs in any one of them may be offset by changes in the others or may be reflected in changes in member bank reserves. The discussion has also brought out how Federal Reserve operations may be adjusted to changes in the various factors affecting bank reserves.

Students of monetary and banking developments can gain considerable insight into the developments of any particular period by arranging and analyzing the monetary factors in terms of the bank reserve equation. The data for these factors are published each month in the *Federal Reserve Bulletin*.

CHAPTER XIII

SHORT-TERM CHANGES IN BANK RESERVES. *Reserve banking policy responds to all of the elements that affect member bank reserve positions. A full accounting of bank reserve factors is published each week in a table accompanying the Reserve Bank condition statement.*

DISCUSSION of the bank reserve equation in Chapter XII dealt with the factors—gold, currency in circulation, and Federal Reserve credit—that have been central in longer-run changes in the general level of member bank reserves. Significant short-run or week-to-week changes in the reserve position can be caused by still other elements, such as changes in Treasury checking accounts, in foreign deposits with the Reserve Banks, and in Federal Reserve float; the latter is an element of Federal Reserve credit that shows substantial week-to-week variation but changes little over the longer run. Operations of the Federal Reserve System must be as responsive to transient as to more lasting reserve changes.

From the standpoint of an observer of day-to-day credit

market conditions or a participant in the market, the fact that member bank reserves have changed is of paramount interest. But how the change came about — that is, what specific factors caused it — is of only slightly less interest to him. Since he is trying to judge the current course of Federal Reserve policy, it is important to him whether a given short-run change is the result of a positive banking action, or reserve banking tolerance of the play of market forces, or of a chance interplay of factors without policy significance.

From the standpoint of its own operations, the Federal Reserve must have detailed knowledge of the performance characteristics and potentialities for fluctuation of each reserve factor, and for this purpose it must maintain a full statistical record of each reserve element. Such background information makes it possible for the System to identify, within a fairly narrow margin of error, the nature and likely amount of prospective changes in the various reserve factors and to decide whether resulting changes in member bank reserves should be permitted or should be offset by System action. As is true of any dynamic process, the administration of policy with regard to the level of member bank reserves must work with a margin of tolerance for the unpredictable, because innumerable economic forces are influencing all of the reserve factors.

Interplay of Elements

The weekly statement includes a table showing all of the elements of the reserve equation. Balance sheet data for the Reserve Banks are consolidated with data from certain accounts of the Treasury that relate to its cash holdings and to its currency outstanding, and with data from member banks on their reserve holdings. Thus, the figures reflect the effects of the country's gold and currency flows upon member bank reserve positions.

DETAILED BANK RESERVE EQUATION
(Weekly averages of daily figures. In millions of dollars)

Factor or element	Week ended July 3, 1963	Change from week ended June 26, 1963
Supplying reserve funds:		
Federal Reserve credit:		
U.S. Government securities.........	32,249	+666
Acceptances......................	44	+1
Member bank borrowings..........	329	+95
Float............................	1,651	−203
Total Federal Reserve credit....	34,273	+559
Gold stock........................	15,733	−46
Treasury currency outstanding........	5,587	+5
Total......................	55,593	+518
Absorbing reserve funds:		
Currency in circulation..............	[1]32,589	+363
Treasury cash holdings..............	390	−12
Deposits with Reserve Banks:		
Treasury........................	863	−29
Foreign..........................	173	−12
Other............................	235	+18
Other Federal Reserve accounts (net)..	1,101	+2
Total......................	35,352	+331
Total reserves held..................	[2]20,241	+188
Required.....................	19,811	+136
Excess.......................	430	+52

[1] Consists of $35,574 million of currency outside the Treasury and Federal Reserve, minus $2,985 million vault cash at member banks.
[2] Of this amount, $17,257 million was held with Reserve Banks and $2,985 million as vault cash at member banks.
NOTE.—Details may not add to totals because of rounding.

217

The weekly reserve equation focuses on how much the member banks have in their reserve accounts. Since it is an average rather than the level on any single day that is significant, the figures for member bank reserves used in the weekly reserve equation are averages of daily figures. The figures for the week ending July 3, 1963, are given in the table on the preceding page.

The information is grouped under two headings—factors supplying reserve funds and factors absorbing reserve funds, with details concerning member bank reserve positions under the latter. For elements supplying reserve funds, increases add to member bank reserves and decreases reduce such reserves. For elements absorbing reserves, increases reduce member bank reserves, and decreases increase them. To highlight the role of particular elements and groups of elements in that week and to facilitate discussion of them, the factors have been rearranged as shown in the following table.

Identifying the Factors in Reserve Changes

At the outset, it should be noted that no great significance can be attached to the changes occurring in a single week, except as they may seem to be part of some longer-term movement. Any week's figures may be affected by fairly wide fluctuations of an unpredictable and short-run nature in such monetary factors as those discussed here.

The most important factors increasing member bank reserves during the week chosen for illustration were increases in some components of Federal Reserve credit, chiefly an increase in U.S. Government securities held by the Federal Reserve. But, setting these particular factors aside for the moment, other factors increasing reserves included decreases in Treasury and foreign deposits at the Reserve Banks.

The changes in Treasury deposits with Federal Reserve Banks reflected Treasury payments for Government ex-

REARRANGEMENT OF
DETAILED BANK RESERVE EQUATION
(Averages of daily figures. In millions of dollars)

Factor or element	Change, June 26 to July 3, 1963[1]
A. Changes accounting for increases in bank reserves:	
Increases in:	
U.S. Government securities held by Reserve Banks.	666
Acceptances held by the Reserve Banks..........	1
Member bank borrowings at Reserve Banks......	95
Treasury currency outstanding.................	5
Decreases in:	
Treasury cash holdings.......................	12
Treasury deposits with Reserve Banks...........	29
Foreign deposits with Reserve Banks...........	12
Total...................................	820
B. Changes accounting for decreases in bank reserves:	
Decreases in:	
Float..	203
Gold stock..................................	46
Increases in:	
Currency in circulation[2].....................	363
Other deposits with Reserve Banks.............	18
Other Federal Reserve accounts (net)...........	2
Total...................................	632
C. Increase in total reserves held (A − B)............	188

[1] Changes based on averages for the weeks ending on these dates.
[2] Outside the Treasury, Federal Reserve, and member banks.

219

penditures made by drawing checks against Treasury accounts with the Federal Reserve Banks. Treasury transactions run into billions of dollars each month. Despite careful supervision of its accounts, Treasury balances at the Reserve Banks often fluctuate abruptly, with corresponding effects (in the opposite direction) on member bank reserves. Over the illustrative week, however, changes in these balances were quite moderate, adding $29 million to reserve funds.

When payments are made out of foreign accounts at the Reserve Banks, the recipients of the payments usually deposit them with member banks, which then add them to reserve accounts at the Reserve Banks. Conversely, when foreign deposits are being built up, there is a corresponding drain on member bank reserves. The decrease in foreign deposits supplied $12 million of reserves in the week under review.

The major factors absorbing reserves in the illustrative week were an increase in currency in circulation and a reduction in Federal Reserve float. There was also a small change in the gold stock.

The public's holdings of currency fluctuate sharply with seasonal spending patterns. The public obtains currency by withdrawing funds from banks, and this reduces bank reserves. When customers return currency to banks, this builds up reserves. During the week under discussion, the public obtained $363 million of currency from banks, thereby reducing bank reserves to that extent.

Federal Reserve float, as explained in Chapter XI, represents Federal Reserve credit extended to member banks through the check collection process, when checks not yet collected by the Federal Reserve are credited to member bank reserve accounts in accordance with an established schedule. The amount of float fluctuates from day to day, primarily in consequence of variations in the volume of check transactions but also as a result of weather and other factors affecting the speed of collection. In our reference week a reduction in float absorbed $203 million of reserve funds.

The U.S. gold stock tends to fluctuate in line with conditions in our international balance of payments. As explained in Chapter VIII, inflows of gold from foreign countries are generally associated with a balance favorable to the United States, while outflows of gold are associated with a balance favorable to foreign countries. During the illustrative week, the gold stock of the United States declined by $46 million.

These factors absorbing reserves were much stronger than factors supplying reserves, other than Federal Reserve credit. Therefore, the Federal Reserve purchased a large amount of U.S. Government securities—$666 million —to keep bank reserves from declining. In addition, member banks on their own increased their reserves another $95 million by borrowing that much from the Federal Reserve Banks.

As a result of all the changes in the various factors— those outside the control of the Federal Reserve System or of member banks and those that reflect Federal Reserve or member bank initiative—total reserves of member banks increased by $188 million.

Total reserves of member banks are divided between required and excess reserves. For the week here reviewed required reserves increased by $136 million, and excess reserves by $52 million.

Meaning of Net Reserve Position

One of the things that the credit market observes in gauging the emphasis of current monetary policy—that is, whether it is tending to be stimulative, neutral, or restrain-

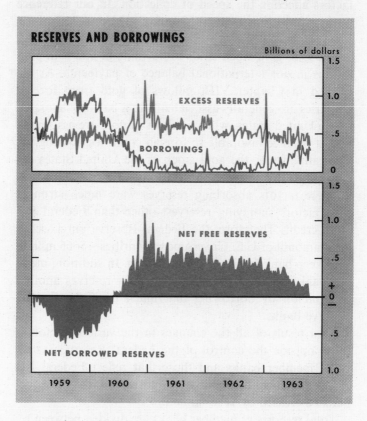

RESERVES AND BORROWINGS

Billions of dollars

EXCESS RESERVES

BORROWINGS

NET FREE RESERVES

NET BORROWED RESERVES

1959 1960 1961 1962 1963

ing in its effects upon the volume of credit and money—is the trend of changes in the net reserve position of member banks. The net reserve position is defined as the dif-

222

ference between the excess reserves of member banks and member bank borrowing; excess reserves, of course, represent the difference between total and required reserves.

The term "net free reserves" is used by the market to refer to a position in which excess reserves are larger than borrowings, while the term "net borrowed reserves" refers to a position in which borrowings are larger than excess reserves. As monetary policy moves from a restraining to a stimulative posture, a net borrowed reserve position will gradually give way to a net free position. These swings in the reserve position usually reflect changes in member bank borrowings more than changes in excess reserves. The reason for this is that banks universally seek to avoid unemployed funds, thus keeping to minimal levels their combined excess reserves and the fluctuations in these reserves.

Referring again to the principal elements in the bank reserve equation for the week ending July 3, 1963, member banks showed net free reserves of $101 million, the amount by which their excess reserves of $430 million exceeded their borrowing of $329 million. Free reserves declined by $43 million from the preceding week (since borrowings were increased by $95 million while excess reserves increased by only $52 million). The member banks' net reserve position over that period appears to have moved in the direction of less monetary ease.

While monetary policy necessarily influences the net reserve position of banks, this position is also much affected by bank responses to the many cross currents that stem from the interplay of diverse market forces and by unforeseen developments. Considering the complexity of the forces affecting the net reserve position in the short run—a fact reflected in the many sizable and irregular fluctuations in this measure from week to week—little or no signifi-cance can be attached to the shift during a single week. However, the downward trend in net free reserves over a period of several months preceding this particular week confirmed that Federal Reserve policy had been tending to become somewhat less stimulative with regard to the growth of credit and money than it had been earlier.

In general, the net reserve position of member banks is an important gauge of pressures on bank reserves. When net free reserves rise, the result is an increased marginal availability of reserves, which the banking system can readily use to expand credit. But when member bank borrowings grow relative to excess reserves, credit ex-pansion comes under restraint. In this process individual banks find extra reserves more difficult and expensive to obtain, and they come under increasing pressure to repay advances from the Federal Reserve. As this continues over time, a net borrowed reserve position emerges for the banking system as a whole.

Of course, the net reserve position of banks is only one index of credit and monetary tendencies and of the di-rection of reserve banking policy, and in this respect it has to be considered in relation to banks' desires to hold free reserves and to other fundamental indicators of credit con-ditions. The central task of monetary policy is to regulate expansion in bank reserves, bank credit, and money so that growth in real output is accomplished with a minimum of either inflationary or deflationary pressures. Changes in bank credit and money, along with other changes in credit, the flow of savings, and interest rates, are among key indices of the credit situation in the short as well as in the longer run.

224

CHAPTER XIV

ORGANIZATION FOR MONETARY POLICY. *The Board of Governors has a central role in achieving coordinated use of all of the instruments of monetary policy, and it maintains close relations with other policy-making agencies in the Government. Federal Reserve Banks play an important part in System policy through representation on the Federal Open Market Committee and through their responsibilities for discount operations.*

D ECISIONS affecting the availability and cost of member bank reserves are made by the Federal Reserve System in light of the many factors—economic, financial, balance of payments, and technical—that have been discussed in earlier chapters. These decisions are the essence of monetary policy. The Federal Reserve System is organized in such a way that monetary policy reflects the considered judgment of the Board of Governors in Washington and the twelve Federal Reserve Banks.

The Board of Governors is a public regulatory body that has a central responsibility for the coordinated use of the various instruments of monetary policy. Its members are appointed by the President with the advice and consent of the Senate. The Federal Reserve Banks, distributed as they are throughout the United States, help to increase the System's responsiveness to local and regional business and credit conditions. Views of the Board and the Banks are exchanged regularly through meetings of the Federal Open Market Committee, at which policy for open market operations is decided. Such operations are the focal point of the day-to-day policy process.

This chapter discusses how the Federal Reserve System is organized to make decisions for monetary policy, while the following chapter goes into considerable detail on the open market policy process, from policy formulation to execution.

Distribution of Federal Reserve Authority

A graphic view of the organization of the Federal Reserve System can be helpful to an understanding of its structure in relation to its primary functions. The chart on page 22 of Chapter II shows in broad outline the statutory organization of the System. The chart on the facing page completes the story on structure by showing the relationship of the organizational parts of the System to the several instruments of credit policy. The four squares at the bottom of the chart represent these instruments; each is joined by a line to the unit or units within the System that make policy decisions with reference to that instrument.

Board of Governors

The Board participates in all of the principal monetary actions of the Federal Reserve System. It has full authority over changes in reserve requirements within the limits

226

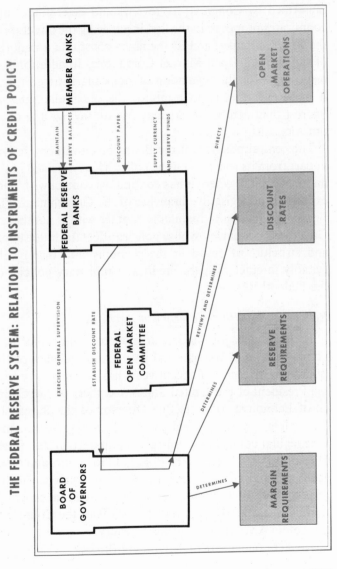

THE FEDERAL RESERVE SYSTEM: RELATION TO INSTRUMENTS OF CREDIT POLICY

MEMBER BANKS

FEDERAL RESERVE BANKS

FEDERAL OPEN MARKET COMMITTEE

BOARD OF GOVERNORS

MAINTAIN RESERVE BALANCES

DISCOUNT PAPER

SUPPLY CURRENCY AND RESERVE FUNDS

EXERCISES GENERAL SUPERVISION

ESTABLISH DISCOUNT RATE

REVIEWS AND DETERMINES

DETERMINES

DIRECTS

DETERMINES

OPEN MARKET OPERATIONS

DISCOUNT RATES

RESERVE REQUIREMENTS

MARGIN REQUIREMENTS

prescribed by Congress; it "reviews and determines" discount rates proposed in the first instance by the directors of the Reserve Banks; and its members constitute a majority of the Federal Open Market Committee. In addition it is responsible for the regulation of stock market credit, and it has the authority to establish the maximum rates of interest that member banks may pay on savings and other time deposits.

The central position of the Board of Governors derives in part from its role as a public policy agency located in the nation's capital, where it has continuous contact with both executive and legislative branches of the Government. The Board of Governors maintains contact with a number of Government agencies, whose policies affect the total supply and structure of credit in the economy and thereby inevitably interact with the credit and monetary policies of the Federal Reserve.

Relations with Other Government Agencies

To facilitate coordination of monetary and other economic policies at the national level, the Chairman of the Board of Governors in recent years has met regularly with the President of the United States, members of the Council of Economic Advisers, the Director of the Bureau of the Budget, and the Secretary of the Treasury. At the same time regular contact has also been maintained at staff levels of responsibility between the Board of Governors and other economic and credit agencies of the Government. In this respect there is continuous exchange of relevant information between the Board's staff and staffs of the Council of Economic Advisers and of the Treasury.

The debt management activities of the U.S. Treasury are

most closely related to monetary policy on a day-to-day basis. Informal contact with Treasury officials at the staff level is fairly continuous. In addition, officials of the two agencies get together for luncheons twice each week to discuss developments and plans. A Monday luncheon, held at the Treasury, is attended by the Secretary of the Treasury, the Chairman or Vice Chairman of the Board of Governors, and Treasury staff advisers. A Wednesday luncheon, held at the Federal Reserve, is attended by the Chairman and Vice Chairman of the Board of Governors, the Under Secretary of the Treasury in charge of debt management and international monetary affairs together with his principal staff assistants, and staff economists of the Board. These points of contact keep the officials of each agency informed of developments that might affect their operations.

In its refunding and borrowing operations the Treasury goes repeatedly to the credit market, where conditions reflect in part the credit and monetary policy of the Federal Reserve. It is important to the Treasury to have a well functioning and resilient market for Government securities, and it is important for the implementation of monetary policy that Treasury financing operations interfere as little as possible with Federal Reserve actions regarding the flow of credit and money.

Certain conditions in the credit market can at times be encouraged through complementary Treasury and Federal Reserve operations. For instance, Treasury management of the debt in the early 1960's helped to keep domestic short-term interest rates from falling to levels that would add to the continuing balance of payments deficit by encouraging further outflows of liquid capital. The Treasury's efforts to this end, in addition, made it easier for the Federal Reserve to maintain a stimulative, easy money policy to foster domestic economic expansion.

With both the Treasury and the Federal Reserve now operating in foreign exchange markets, and with both agencies participating regularly with their counterparts in other countries in international discussions that involve policy proposals, the need for close coordination of Federal Reserve and Treasury operations in the international sphere too has increased greatly. This involves continuous exchange of information among principals at the Treasury, the Board of Governors, and the Federal Reserve Bank of New York, and this information is also made available to other Reserve Banks.

With regard to international financial problems in general, the Chairman of the Board of Governors is a member of the National Advisory Council on International Monetary and Financial Problems, which includes in its membership the heads of all agencies that make foreign loans or engage in foreign financial transactions.

Federal Reserve Banks

In the administration of monetary policy, Federal Reserve Banks play a principal role in discount operations of the System. In fact, the setting of discount rates and the administration of discounting operations provide an excellent illustration of the ways in which decision-making responsibilities are shared in the decentralized Federal Reserve System.

Establishment of the discount rate is one of the main responsibilities of the directors of the Federal Reserve Banks. Every fourteen days the directors of each Bank must establish a discount rate subject to review and determination by the Board of Governors in Washington. This procedure assures that regional conditions and credit needs as well as national and international conditions are taken into account in setting the rate.

These broader national and international considerations are sometimes reflected differently or have different degrees of importance in the various regions of the country. Hence, at times there are diverse views as to the proper movement of discount rates. In general, however, economic tendencies and credit conditions tend to be more or less national in character, and opinions as to desirable changes in discount rates usually are quite similar.

The Reserve Banks have full responsibility for deciding what loans and discounts to individual member banks are consistent with the Federal Reserve Act. The objectives of the Act, however, are interpreted by the Board of Governors in its Regulation A, quoted on page 43. Regulation A, as explained in Chapter III, sets the general conditions under which discount accommodation will be granted to member banks. Within these guidelines, there are a few differences in practice from one Reserve Bank to another that stem from the different traditions, customs, and basic economic structures of various regions of the country. But the general standards governing discounting are the same for all Reserve districts.

The total volume of loans and advances made to member banks varies over the economic cycle as the pressure of credit demand on the available supply of member bank reserves changes. However, the guiding principles of Regulation A, which govern the granting of credit to individual member banks, do not so change. Thus, in discount administration the only element that is adjusted as policy objectives change is the discount rate.

In addition to their role in discount administration, Reserve Banks participate in the formulation and execution of policy for open market operations as discussed in following paragraphs.

Federal Open Market Committee

As pointed out in an earlier chapter, the Federal Open Market Committee consists of the seven members of the Board of Governors together with the presidents of five of the Reserve Banks. The Chairman of the Board of Governors serves as Chairman of the Committee, and the President of the Federal Reserve Bank of New York serves as Vice Chairman. The President of the New York Bank is a permanent member of the Committee. Presidents of the other Banks rotate as members, with four being elected by the Reserve Banks voting in groups prescribed by law. Membership of these four is for one year.

The presidents of all the Reserve Banks participate in discussions at the meetings, although only those who are currently members vote on proposed Committee actions. In this way the knowledge and information of the entire Federal Reserve System is available to the Committee. At the same time it helps to keep all Reserve Bank officials informed about present thinking on general monetary policy and about developments in the domestic and world economies.

The Open Market Committee meets often — generally every three weeks. This permits a continual interchange of ideas and evaluation of the latest economic and financial developments. At each meeting the Committee, with the help of its staff, reviews the national and international business and credit situation.

Decisions about open market policy and the coordination of open market operations with other instruments of monetary policy are thus made in the light of a full and continuing discussion of regional, national, and international conditions. In this sense, the Federal Open Market Committee is the focal point for formulation of Federal Reserve monetary policy.

Operations in Government securities and in foreign currencies that are authorized by the Federal Open Market Committee are undertaken by the Federal Reserve Bank of New York for the System Open Market Account. The Manager of the Account supervises all domestic security transactions, and the Special Manager supervises all operations in foreign currencies. Both the Manager and the Special Manager, in addition to being officials of the Federal Open Market Committee, are officers of the Federal Reserve Bank of New York. All transactions executed by them are in accordance with the Committee's instructions. Each Reserve Bank participates in holdings and earnings of the System Account.

To facilitate the execution of operations in Government securities and foreign currencies, the System Account Management maintains trading rooms at the Federal Reserve Bank of New York. These are linked by telephone to the major dealers in the Government securities and foreign exchange markets. In addition to being used for transacting System business, the trading rooms serve as listening posts, which permit both the Manager and the Special Manager to keep in close touch with changes in market conditions and market psychology.

233

Against this organizational background, the next chapter explains the role and workings of the Open Market Committee and the System Open Market Account Management in the formulation and execution of monetary policy—in particular open market operations, for which they have direct responsibility.

CHAPTER XV

THE OPEN MARKET POLICY PROCESS. *In deciding on reserve banking policy, account must be taken of all the economic forces at work in the domestic economy as well as of those affecting relations with the rest of the world. Complexities of the economic situation require that reserve banking instruments be used flexibly, with the nature of the banking process making for central reliance on open market operations. As a result, the formulation of open market policy and the conduct of operations in the market are at the heart of the policy process.*

THE process by which reserve banking policy influences the economy begins with changes in the availability and cost of member bank reserves. The Federal Reserve can initiate such changes through its open market operations, through changes in the rate at which it discounts paper for banks, and—within limits—through changes in the reserve requirements of member banks.

Changes in the availability and cost of reserves are reflected immediately in money market conditions. Their influence spreads to bank credit and money, to interest rates in markets for longer-term debt, and to the entire range of spending financed by borrowed funds. In the end the ultimate targets of policy actions—total income and spending, total output and employment, the general level of prices, and international trade and capital flows—come to be influenced.

At all times, however, financial conditions, domestic economic activity, and the balance of international payments are influenced by many underlying forces that make themselves felt independently of monetary actions. Thus, while the Federal Reserve undertakes to direct its policy toward attainment of orderly economic progress and a stable dollar, these objectives cannot be reached through monetary policy alone.

Complexities of Policy-Making

The policy process in reserve banking involves a continuing assessment of changing economic developments and takes full account of the interaction of monetary measures and forces outside the monetary sphere. For instance, when the performance of the economy or of the balance of international payments has been falling short of longer-range objectives, Federal Reserve authorities must decide whether and to what extent changes in the financial variables more directly affected by monetary action—namely, the pace of bank credit and monetary growth, and levels of interest rates—can help to improve the situation. They must also decide whether changes in other forces—including other public policies—are working or may work to remedy the shortfall. If it seems appropriate to change the pace at which bank credit and the money supply are growing or to change prevailing interest rates, then the policy-makers must decide by how much and with what timing to adjust the reserve base of member banks so that monetary action will encourage the change desired.

Judgments of this kind call for full analysis of all relevant information about the domestic economic and credit situation, the flows being generated in international payments, and the major forces affecting the world economy generally. Hence in arriving at policy decisions the Federal Reserve considers a spectrum of guides. These range from ultimate goals for output, employment, average prices, and the balance of payments to the more immediate objectives, such as bank reserve availability, which transmit System policy to money market conditions and interest rates, bank credit, and the money supply.

It would be easier for the System to make decisions on policy if there were a simple statistical norm—such as a particular rate of growth in the money supply or particular levels of interest rates—which, if it could be attained, might insure continuous realization of optimum conditions in output, employment, and the balance of payments. Neither experience nor a consensus of economic theory, however, has indicated any single norm for policy guidance. Rather, the Federal Reserve System must consider changes in all indicators, financial and nonfinancial, that help to explain recent economic tendencies, that shed light on likely future developments, and that reflect the stance of monetary policy in relation to other influences on the economy.

Policy-makers thus place a high priority on comprehensive, dependable, and timely economic intelligence. A wide range of information, both statistical and qualitative, is available for use in making such judgments, and methods of economic analysis are much advanced over those used in earlier periods.

Even so, opinions differ on how the available information should be interpreted. These differences arise because there are still important gaps in the data and because the information that is available currently does not fully reveal emerging economic developments in the domestic and international spheres. In addition, different participants in the decision-making process may attach different weights to the various elements in an evolving situation—not only among domestic factors but as between domestic and international.

In this complex economic world—in which data tend to run somewhat behind events and in which the effects of changes in Federal Reserve policy work themselves out over time—adaptations in policy tend to be taken step by step. In that way, they can be readily modified or reversed, if necessary, as the future unfolds. This is especially important at times when the strength of perceivable trends is not clear or when there is strong interaction between domestic and international economic developments. Nevertheless, situations may arise that clearly call for rapid and forceful policy measures. In these circumstances, too, the continuous nature of the policy process permits prompt response.

Role of the Open Market Committee

In view of the way in which the U.S. banking system is structured and the way in which banking processes have evolved, open market operations are the instrument best suited to step-by-step adaptation of monetary policy. They can be used to initiate small policy actions or aggressively to carry out large changes in reserves over relatively short periods. They are continuous in nature, can be undertaken quickly, and are well adapted to ready modification and reversal, if necessary. In practice, therefore, open market operations normally take the lead in general monetary policy implementation, with changes in the discount rate and in required reserve ratios being used more often to supplement and reinforce this initiative.

All of the System's open market operations—in both domestic securities and foreign currencies—are carried out under policy directives of the Federal Open Market Committee. The Committee's procedures and practices have varied over the years along with the changing focus of the issues and problems faced. The practices described in following paragraphs are those that have evolved out of past experience to meet present needs. As needs change in the future and as knowledge increases further, current practices are likely to be modified.

To keep open market policy constantly in touch with the monetary and credit needs of the economy and with the international economic position of the country, the Committee has found it essential to meet often, usually every three weeks. The primary purpose of these meetings is to develop a policy consensus that can be formulated into operating directives to the Manager of the System Open Market Account and the Special Manager for foreign currency operations. The meetings are also a forum for discussion of the use of all instruments of monetary policy against the background of over-all monetary objectives.

Decisions on changes in the use of policy instruments other than open market operations—discount rates and reserve requirements—are not made by the Federal Open

Market Committee as such. But since all policy instruments are closely related, views developed in Committee deliberations are carried over into meetings of the Board of Governors and of the Reserve Bank presidents with their directors, where actions on these other instruments are decided. In this way Committee discussions have a bearing on the coordinated use of all instruments.

Committee Procedures

Meetings of the Federal Open Market Committee are organized to facilitate wide discussion and careful assessment of available information as part of the process of coming to decisions on open market policy. To this end, all twelve of the Reserve Bank presidents attend the meetings and participate in the discussion, although only the five who are members vote on proposed Committee actions. This arrangement makes the knowledge and information of the entire Federal Reserve System available to the Committee.

Background preparation. Between meetings, members of the Committee are kept informed about late developments in the nation's economy, in regional economies, and in the balance of payments by the research staffs at the Board of Governors and at each of the Reserve Banks. Regular briefings are provided in both oral and written form. Some of these staff reports stress only the facts of recent changes. Others assess and interpret them in relation to past trends and in terms of the key factors in economic cycles and growth suggested by various economic theories. Such analyses are helpful in the assessment of possible future trends.

In addition, Committee members receive regular reports

240

from the Manager of the System Open Market Account and the Special Manager for foreign currency operations. These reports—provided daily, weekly, and in advance of each meeting—analyze developments in the domestic money and securities markets, in bank reserve positions, and in foreign exchange markets. They also provide a full review of System operations against the background of Committee objectives.

Before each meeting members of the Committee receive special staff reports that place developments since the preceding meeting in clear perspective. One of these is a review of the key phases of the current economic situation, domestic and international, prepared by the research staff of the Board of Governors. It sets forth recent information on the broad economic aggregates that represent the ultimate targets of domestic policy—output, employment, income, and prices—and reviews changes in such important factors as business investment, housing, consumer outlays, and Government finance that underlie movements in these broad aggregates. In addition, it reviews developments in key financial variables such as bank credit, money, and interest rates, which are the proximate targets of policy, and reports changes in the money market and bank reserve statistics that respond most immediately to monetary policy actions. Finally, it sets forth summary information on output and credit conditions abroad and the state of the U.S. balance of payments. When special problems or proposals relating to policy are under consideration, Committee members usually receive supplementary background papers.

Organization. Meetings of the Federal Open Market Committee are held at the Board of Governors building in

241

Washington. The agenda for each meeting is typically divided into two parts. One focuses on foreign currency operations; the other on broader questions of general open market policy.

The discussion of foreign currency operations begins with an oral report by the Special Manager of the Account. He reviews the highlights of recent foreign exchange market experience and identifies situations likely to require Committee attention or action before the next meeting. After discussion of questions raised by his comments and recommendations, the Committee takes whatever actions may be needed to direct foreign currency operations until the next meeting.

The meeting then proceeds to a consideration of general open market policy. Discussion begins with an oral report by the Account Manager. In this he outlines recent and prospective System actions in the market and reviews money and securities market developments expected to be of special significance to the Committee in the period ahead. If Committee members have questions or reservations about the conduct of open market operations in the interval since the last meeting, they raise them at this point.

The Committee then receives oral briefings from its staff economists. These are analytical and interpretive statements that draw out the significance and implications of the more detailed written reports distributed in advance of the meeting. One statement covers key developments in domestic business; another, recent changes in domestic financial markets; and a third, recent developments in the U.S. balance of payments.

After the staff reports, each Board member and Bank

president—nonvoting as well as voting—speaks in turn. Each presents his judgments on current economic and financial conditions, and the Reserve Bank presidents report any significant recent developments in the economies of their districts.

These summaries of regional conditions are useful in interpreting over-all economic tendencies because they often help to spot developments not yet reflected in statistical series for the nation as a whole. Also, reports by the Bank presidents reflect a special knowledge of banking developments obtained from supervision of member banks, administration of the discount window, and other regular contacts with bankers and business leaders, including their Bank's directors.

Each speaker states his view with regard to policy, usually by indicating whether he believes that money market conditions and the volume of reserves available to member banks should be kept about the same or be changed. Recommendations to shift toward more or less ease or restraint in open market operations may include an expression of opinion as to the desirability of a near-term change in the discount rate. In addition, speakers typically relate any proposals they may have concerning money market conditions and bank reserves to broader financial variables such as interest rates, the pace of bank credit and monetary growth, or other liquid assets. They also assess these financial variables against trends in domestic economic activity and employment, the level of prices, and the balance of international payments. When all members of the Committee have spoken, the Chairman summarizes the points of view expressed and the consensus that seems to have developed on open market policy.

243

Following such further comments as may help to clarify differing points of view, attention turns to the current policy directive, which expresses the Committee's judgment as to the appropriate posture of monetary policy for the period until the next meeting. If the policy judgment that is reached calls for a change in the directive, alternative formulations are considered. Then a vote of the Committee members is taken on that policy formulation which seems to express most satisfactorily the majority view. On occasion the wording of the directive will be revised to acknowledge the short-run significance of some unexpected event or condition such as the Suez crisis in late 1956, the stock market break in May 1962, the Cuban crisis in October 1962, or President Kennedy's assassination in November 1963. Developments of this type may be deemed to require specific recognition in the policy directive, even though basic policy remains unchanged.

The directives of the Federal Open Market Committee to the System Account Managers provide the central basis for the record of Committee policy actions published in the *Annual Reports* of the Board of Governors. But more fundamentally they establish formal lines of policy direction from the 12-member policy-forming Committee to the Account Managers, who execute day-to-day market operations. Thus, the directives, discussed in the next section, are the basis for policy execution, although the Managers' understanding of the instructions is enhanced by their presence at the Committee's discussions.

Execution of Policy

Over its history the Committee has changed the form of its directives from time to time. At present, instructions for open market operations in domestic securities are contained in two directives. One is a "continuing authority directive," which is reviewed at least once a year. It sets the technical limits on operations—indicating such things as the types of securities that may be bought or sold, the procedures to be followed in transactions, and the conditions under which repurchase agreements may be made with dealers. The other is the current policy directive voted at each meeting. This states the present objectives of open market policy and gives guidance, in light of the Committee's discussions, to the Account Manager in implementing Committee policy until the next meeting.

The current policy directive is revised rather often. Revisions take account of recent and prospective changes in the domestic economy and the balance of payments, which may require alterations in open market policy.

With regard to foreign currency operations, the policy aims of the Committee relate to the international position of the dollar as mirrored in the technical performance of foreign exchange markets and to the way in which the deficit or surplus in the U.S. balance of payments is financed. When the Open Market Committee authorized operations in foreign currencies in 1962, it defined the goals and character of this program in a detailed statement. The statement, published by the Board in its *Annual Report* for 1962, explained the purposes of foreign currency operations, the types of currencies in which transactions could be conducted, the nature of institutional arrangements with central banks in other countries, and the administrative structure and procedures to be used for executing transactions.

At the same time the Committee adopted a set of guidelines for foreign currency operations. These define the circumstances in which the System may acquire and hold foreign currencies and specify the purposes for which it may engage in spot and forward exchange transactions. These rules guide the Special Manager in his day-to-day operations in foreign currencies. A continuing authority directive, subject to change when appropriate, lists the particular foreign currencies in which he may operate, along with the quantitative limits on various types of transactions.

At least once a year—at its annual organization meeting in early March—the Federal Open Market Committee reviews all of its continuing directives and operating procedures to make sure they are consistent with the present needs and objectives of effective monetary policy.

The balance of this article discusses the factors taken into account in the wording of the current policy directive and in the execution of day-to-day open market operations in domestic securities.

The operating problem. The main function of the current policy directive is to set forth guidelines as to the availability of member bank reserves and the degree of ease or firmness in the money market for the Account Manager to follow until the next meeting. These objectives have to be expressed in a manner that will give the Account Manager adequate guidance while at the same time allowing him sufficient latitude—in view of continuously evolving market conditions and expectations—to carry out basic Committee aims in relation to domestic economic activity and the balance of payments.

It might seem at first glance as if the Committee could achieve its objectives by simply stating the dollar volume of securities that the Account Manager should buy or sell in the market before the next meeting. In practice, however, this is not feasible, for the supply of reserves available to member banks is affected by changes in a number of factors that in the short run are independent of Federal Reserve monetary action. Among these are changes in the level of monetary gold, currency in circulation, and float—the last arising mainly from fluctuations in the volume of checks in process of collection. As a result the System can bring about a desired change in the general availability of reserves to banks only if reserve changes arising from these other factors have been fully allowed for.

The task of taking into account changes in these factors, together with normal seasonal movements in required reserves, is essentially an operating problem rather than a policy problem. It is a part of the Account Manager's job— with the help of the staffs at the Federal Reserve Bank of New York and the Board of Governors—to detect such variations and to make prompt adjustments to them. In other words, the execution of open market policy requires a continuous and sensitive appraisal of day-to-day market conditions.

Looking ahead to the interval between meetings, the Committee itself cannot easily predict the amount of reserves that open market operations will have to supply or absorb to take account of changes in other factors affecting reserves. But as the period unfolds, the Account Manager can usually accommodate his operations to such changes. He may observe the changes through statistical measures developed by the staff, or they may become evident to him in the process of day-to-day operations in the money market. Most open market transactions are undertaken simply to respond to seasonal and other short-term reserve changes of these kinds.

For policy purposes the Federal Open Market Committee is less interested in the gross volume of open market transactions likely to be needed in the period ahead than it is in the supply of reserves that will be available to support further growth of bank credit at member banks.

Several measures help to indicate the extent of reserve availability at member banks. For measuring the results of policy actions over a period of weeks or months, trends in total, required, and nonborrowed reserves are particularly useful, because they reveal changes in the reserve base that supports bank deposit and credit expansion. But these measures have only limited usefulness as very short-run operating guides for the System Account Manager—and it is in the short run that day-to-day operations must be planned and executed. To be used effectively on a day-to-day basis, these measures would have to be adjusted to allow for immediate seasonal pressures on reserves as well as for other short-run forces that may unexpectedly produce a sudden bulging or slackening of reserve needs. Such adjustments are difficult at best, and for current operations in such a complex and dynamic economy as that of the United States where it is hard to find recurring patterns, they have to be viewed as tentative or approximate.

In the very short run various marginal measures of bank reserve positions are useful indicators of the interaction between monetary policy and market forces. These indicators include the amounts of excess reserves that member banks hold and the amounts of their borrowings from the Federal Reserve. Subtraction of total member bank borrowings from their total excess reserves provides a net measure of reserve positions for all member banks. As explained in Chapter XIII, when this difference is positive, it is popularly referred to as net free reserves; when it is negative, it is called net borrowed reserves.

The technical advantage of marginal reserve guides is that they help the Account Manager to accommodate seasonal and other short-run credit demands readily as they develop. For example, when net reserves are tending to fall because of a seasonal or random rise in the public's need for bank credit, the Account Manager will supply the reserves required to back the deposits created in credit expansion. Similarly, when net reserves are tending to rise because of a seasonal decline in the demand for bank credit—taking the form, for example, of seasonal repayment of bank debt by business—he will absorb the required reserves released by the associated decline in deposits. With smaller deposits, banks would need less required reserves and their excess reserves would rise unless absorbed by System operations.

Taken by itself, however, the net free (or net borrowed) reserve position also has limitations as a guide. For one thing, it may not show what is happening to total bank credit over time. A given level of net reserves at one point may be associated with a faster or slower rate of growth in total bank credit than the same level of net reserves at another time because of differences in the strength of credit demand, the level and structure of interest rates, and market expectations — all of which affect bank preferences for free reserves.

The danger in adhering to net reserves alone as a guide is that the System might be misled into reinforcing changing demands for bank credit generated by forces of cycli-

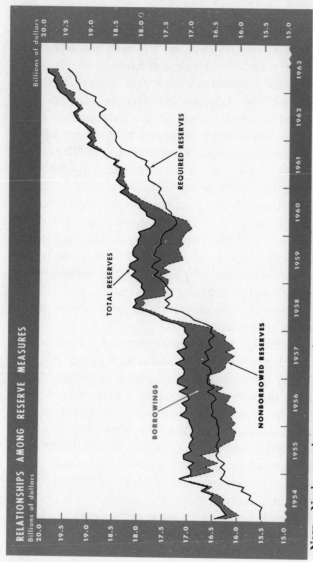

RELATIONSHIPS AMONG RESERVE MEASURES

NOTE.—Nonborrowed reserves are total reserves less member bank borrowings. The difference between nonborrowed reserves and required reserves is the net reserve position of the banking system. Thus, when non-borrowed reserves exceed required reserves, member banks as a group have net free reserves, but when nonborrowed fall below required, member banks as a group have a net borrowed reserve position.

cal expansion and contraction when this was undesirable. For example, in periods of vigorous credit demands and rising bank needs for reserves, free reserves tend to decline as banks use reserves that formerly had been excess or increase their borrowings from Federal Reserve Banks. If in such circumstances there were additions to the total supply of bank reserves through open market operations in order to keep free reserves from falling, this would encourage a rapid expansion of bank credit—perhaps more rapid than desired to accommodate the seasonal, cyclical, and growth needs at the time.

Under conditions of slack credit demands and declining interest rates, on the other hand, the opposite may occur. In such periods member banks typically try to repay debt at the Federal Reserve and add to their excess reserves in an effort to build up their free reserves. If, in these circumstances, free reserves within the banking system were not permitted to grow enough to meet the changed preferences, open market operations would tend to encourage further contraction rather than the credit expansion that would help stimulate economic recovery. In short, although the net reserve measure is a useful and sensitive short-run guide to open market operations, it is not used inflexibly as a policy target. Rather, it is continuously interpreted in the light of other evidence on credit and economic developments and in the light of changes in various fundamental measures of the bank reserve base—total, required, and nonborrowed reserves.

Moreover, even in the short run the significance of any given net reserve figure must be assessed alongside a broad assortment of other information that bears on what is typically alluded to as the "tone" or "feel" of the money

251

market. Indicators such as the intensity of demand for and the depth of supply of Federal funds, the amount of new money needed by Government securities dealers and their sources and costs of financing, and day-to-day trends in market prices and yields for Treasury securities all provide important insights into the immediate state of reserve availability and the strength of demands pressing upon that availability. In executing policy it is essential to have these immediate indicators of money market atmosphere, because daily estimates of reserve availability may be wide of the mark and because such estimates are for the banking system as a whole and do not allow for the differing market impact of possible variations in reserve distribution.

In summary, although at first glance it might seem to be most efficient for the Federal Open Market Committee to express its instructions to the System Account Manager in simple and explicit terms—either as some dollar amount of net purchases or net sales to be accomplished before the next meeting, or as some given target of net reserve availability or reserve growth—this quantitative approach has not proved feasible. Experience has shown that the Committee cannot forecast the size of technical adjustments that will be needed between meetings to allow for changes in other reserve factors. Nor can it predict the precise extent to which bank credit, money, and interest rates will respond to given target levels of, or changes in, reserve availability.

Nature of operating instructions. In practice, therefore, the Committee finds it desirable to express its operating instructions in broader terms, which allow the Account Manager sufficient latitude to evaluate and interpret changing technical relationships among all of the relevant money market indicators. For this reason Committee instructions have typically directed the Account Manager to seek more, less, or about the same amount of reserve availability and money market ease or tightness as has been prevailing. Decisions as to the precise size, timing, and direction (purchase or sale) of any market operations needed to implement these instructions are left to the Manager's discretion, for he has day-to-day contact with the market and with the daily figures bearing on bank reserves and money market conditions and he is therefore in a position to make the necessary and continuing day-to-day adaptations of operations to basic policy aims.

To illustrate the form of operating instructions, the current economic policy directive adopted at the meeting of September 11, 1962, follows:

It is the current policy of the Federal Open Market Committee to permit the supply of bank credit and money to increase further, but at the same time to avoid redundant bank reserves that would encourage capital outflows internationally. This policy takes into account, on the one hand, the gradualness of recent advance in economic activity and the availability of resources to permit further advance in activity. On the other hand, it gives recognition to the bank credit expansion over the past year and to the role of capital flows in the country's adverse balance of payments.

To implement this policy, operations for the System Open Market Account during the next three weeks shall be conducted with a view to providing moderate reserve expansion in the banking system and to fostering a moderately firm tone in money markets.

In making day-to-day decisions, the Account Manager adheres to the guidelines of the current directive. As the example shows, the first paragraph contains a statement of the Committee's broad goals, and the second its operating instructions.

If changes in banking and money market conditions in the period between meetings should begin to deviate sharply from the general pattern assumed in the policy deliberations at the latest meeting, the Account Manager would call this to the Committee's attention. If the change were very rapid, he might ask for a special meeting (perhaps by telephone conference) to review alternative means of coping with the changed situation and to determine whether the Committee wished to issue new operating instructions. Any Committee member who was similarly concerned by the unexpected course of developments could, of course, also request a special meeting. In fact, Committee members may at any time make comments to the System Account Manager about actual operations of the System Account and market developments in relation to Committee intentions.

Basis for day-to-day operations. In his day-to-day evaluation of money market developments the Account Manager considers both statistical and qualitative measures of financial activity. One key element in this continuous evaluation process is a daily projection of changes in factors affecting bank reserves. The reserve projection contains estimates for several weeks ahead of daily and weekly average changes in all of the key elements that affect the bank reserve equation—float, currency, gold and foreign accounts, and so forth—as well as in the various reserve measures—total, required, nonborrowed, and free reserves. These projections show the direction and general order of magnitude of the open market operations likely to be needed in the period immediately ahead.

Every morning the daily and weekly estimates for factors affecting reserves are revised on the basis of actual reserve figures collected for the preceding business day from the System's statistical reporting network. Since the money market is especially sensitive to the current and expected reserve position of large city banks, figures on the distribution of reserves among banks are also assembled from the reported data and carefully evaluated.

Data on reserves are supplemented by other types of statistical information. For example, statistics on transactions in Federal funds are collected daily from a sample of large money market banks. These shed light on the demand for and supply of excess reserves by banks and are a sensitive indicator of changes in current bank reserve availability relative to the demand for bank credit. In addition, the Account Manager receives from the Market Statistics Department of the Federal Reserve Bank of New York aggregate data collected from Government securities dealers that show their current inventories, volume of trading, and sources of financing.

Apart from these various types of current and retrospective statistics, the Account Manager obtains through a network of telephone contacts maintained by the Trading Desk a wide assortment of information from Government securities dealers and other money market professionals on current rate and price quotations in money markets as well as estimates of customer offerings and demands in markets for Federal funds and U.S. Government securities. This information, which reflects the interaction of the volume of reserves actually available and the demand pressing upon these reserves, is needed for meaningful interpretation and evaluation of the preliminary statistical estimates on bank reserve positions. It also helps the Account Manager to come to a better understanding of market expectations and of the likely response to Federal Reserve operations.

This brief review of the guides and information that

shape day-to-day activities of the Account Manager illustrates the wide range of information he takes into account in the execution of policy. The Manager, in turn, keeps members of the Committee continuously informed of the particular money market and bank reserve developments that underlie each day's actions. Insights gained from these reports of current developments, in combination with analyses of the broader but less timely indicators of general changes in the domestic economy and the balance of payments, provide the background information on which Committee members must base their new policy judgment at the succeeding meeting.

CHAPTER XVI

SUPERVISORY FUNCTIONS OF THE FEDERAL RE-
SERVE. *By keeping individual banks strong and by maintaining competition among banks, bank supervision helps to maintain an adequate and responsive banking system. This contributes
to the effective functioning of monetary policy and of economic
processes generally.*

FOR the general instruments of monetary policy to
work effectively, the nation must have a responsive
banking system in which the public has full confidence.
The orderly functioning of such a system depends on the
effective operation of each bank in the system.

The current financial needs of commerce, industry, and
agriculture are met in part through loans and investments
made by individual banks, and the bulk of the nation's
payments are made through the checking accounts in
these banks. As a factor of instability, failure of banks to
meet their liabilities can reach far beyond depositors and
borrowers and the immediate territory that the banks
serve. The business of banking, therefore, is vested with a

257

public interest and is subject to supervision by governmental authorities.

Bank supervision, which began in this country more than a century ago, is rooted in two characteristics peculiar to the American banking system: first, a large number of commercial banks differing greatly in size and in the type of banking service offered; and second, the wide variety of detailed State and national banking laws and of regulations issued under these laws.

Fundamentally, bank supervision is directed to safeguarding and serving the community's interest. In relation to individual banks, the objective is to foster the maintenance of each in sound and solvent condition and under good management, in order to protect depositors and to assure uninterrupted provision of essential banking services. With respect to all banks, a further objective is to help maintain a banking system which will adapt continuously and responsively to the financial needs of a growing economy and in which individual units will compete actively in rendering banking services.

Compass of Bank Supervision

As a governmental activity, bank supervision encompasses a wide variety of technical functions relating to the operations of banks. These concern the issuance and enforcement of supervisory and other regulations; the organization and chartering of banks; the periodic examination of banks and the requiring of steps by bank management to correct unsatisfactory or unsound conditions found through such examination; the review and analysis of periodic reports of condition and of income and dividends; and the rendering of counsel and advice

258

on bank operating problems when requested, particularly in the case of smaller banks.

In addition, bank supervision deals with approval of proposed changes in the scope of corporate functions exercised by individual banks and of proposed changes in their capital structures; authorization of branches; approval of bank mergers and consolidations; and regulation of bank holding companies.

Bank supervision is concerned primarily with banks as going concerns. Therefore, its principal objective is to protect the banking structure against weakness of the component banks and whenever possible to assist them in becoming stronger units. Another important aim is to prevent undue concentration of banking ownership and power, which could inhibit competition and the availability of adequate alternative banking facilities.

Given these aims, the major responsibility of supervisory authorities is to keep informed of the condition, operations, and management of the banks subject to their review and to contribute to the prevention or correction of situations that, through inadequacy of either banking capability or banking competition, might adversely affect the economy or the general public interest.

Role of Bank Examination

Bank examination is the best known form of supervisory activity. Its purpose is to develop information that will disclose the current financial condition of the individual bank, ascertain whether the bank is complying with applicable laws and regulations, and indicate the bank's future operating prospects. A bank examination is not an audit since as a general practice it does not include detailed checking of entries relating to transactions or direct verification of individual loan and deposit balances. Banks are encouraged to provide such audit facilities through internal audit departments of their own or the services of public accountants.

The bank examiner in the field, therefore, is primarily a fact finder and an appraiser. Examination steps include analysis and appraisal of a bank's assets; analysis of its liabilities; review and appraisal of its management; review of the administration of its trust department activities; determination of its capital and liquidity position and operating trends; study of the bank's position, expectations, and plans in relation to business conditions in the community as well as generally; and consideration of the bank's performance in the light of various statutory and regulatory provisions affecting the conduct of its business.

In the light of examiners' findings, the supervisory authority formulates and expresses the appropriate supervisory policy and prescribes such steps as may need to be taken to correct criticized phases of a bank's affairs. The supervisory policy expressed and the corrective measures prescribed for a particular bank necessarily reflect the composite experience of the supervisory authority in examining and supervising many banks over a period of many years.

Uses of the examination information are fourfold. In the first place the directors and officers of examined banks use it as the basis of action to strengthen their banks as well as to prevent future difficulties. Second, the banking authorities make it the basis of supervisory policy and action with respect to particular institutions, including decisions whether to approve branches, mergers, or competing bank charters. Third, information accumulated from many examinations guides the authorities in framing or revising regulations, in shaping or reshaping supervisory policies, and in recommending necessary or desirable changes in banking laws. Fourth, the intimate knowledge of banking conditions developed in the Federal Reserve System as a result of bank examination and supervision gives monetary policy-makers a greater feeling for prospective shifts in attitudes and expectations of bankers and businessmen. Both the data and the nonstatistical knowledge that are obtained in the examination and supervisory process are an essential part of the nation's economic intelligence.

Governmental Agencies Concerned with Supervision

The complex nature of this country's banking system is reflected in, and is in part the product of, the governmental structure of bank supervision. State banks are chartered by and operate under the laws of any one of the fifty States. National banks in all States and the District of Columbia operate under Federal banking law, with membership in the Federal Reserve System mandatory. System membership is also available to State banks that meet membership qualifications. A system of Federal insurance of deposits is applicable to all member banks and to others that desire and qualify for insurance.

In such a structure of bank supervision there are necessarily cases of overlapping responsibilities and functions. All of the supervisory authorities have similar basic objectives, however, and by cooperating with each other in developing effective working arrangements, they have been able to avoid much of the seeming duplication in activities.

261

Federal Government legislation to deal with banking problems at different times has given rise to three Federal agencies actively and directly engaged in bank supervisory functions:

The Office of the Comptroller of the Currency, a bureau of the Treasury Department established in 1863, has charter and supervisory authority with respect to the national banks of the country.

The Federal Reserve System, established in 1913 to provide, among other purposes, a "more effective supervision of banking in the United States," has supervisory authority with respect to all its members and also with respect to all bank holding companies. In practice, the System confines its field examinations to State member banks and, whenever practicable, it makes such examinations jointly with State supervisory authorities.

The Federal Deposit Insurance Corporation, established in 1933, has supervisory authority in connection with its responsibility to insure deposits of Federal Reserve member banks and of other banks that voluntarily become insured by the Corporation. The Corporation in practice examines only those insured banks that are not subject to examination by another Federal supervisory agency.

Scope of System Supervisory Functions

The supervisory functions of the Federal Reserve are varied. Its responsibilities in this area are concerned particularly with admission of State banks to membership in the System; the field examination of State member banks and review of operations of all member banks; the correction of unsatisfactory conditions in State member banks or of violation of banking law by them, including, if necessary, disciplinary action to remove officers and directors for unsafe or unsound banking practices or for continued violation of banking law; and the issuance and enforcement of regulations pertaining to member banks.

Other Federal Reserve supervisory functions include approval of the establishment of branches or absorption of other banks by State member banks; permission to holding companies to acquire stock of banks and to vote stock in member banks; chartering of foreign banking and financing corporations; granting permission to member banks to engage in banking in foreign countries; and supervision related to regulation of loans by banks, brokers, and dealers in securities for the purpose of purchasing or carrying of stocks registered on national securities exchanges.

In carrying out these functions the Federal Reserve authorities deal with complex and highly technical banking questions. For example, in passing upon an application for approval of a proposed acquisition of bank shares under the Bank Holding Company Act, the Board is required to consider the financial history, condition, and prospects of the institutions concerned; the character of their respective managements; the convenience, needs, and welfare of the communities and area served; and whether or not the effect of the acquisition would be to expand the size or extent of the particular bank holding company system beyond limits that are consistent with adequate and sound banking, the public interest, and the preservation of competition in the field of banking.

Under a policy of decentralization, the Board of Governors has delegated to the Federal Reserve Banks some phases of the field work involved in Federal Reserve supervisory activities, notably the bank examination function. The Board of Governors, however, directs and coordinates the supervisory work of the Reserve Banks, reviews the results of their examination activities, and determines broad supervisory policies.

The Reserve Banks do not examine national banks since the Comptroller of the Currency is directly charged with that responsibility under the law. In this way the two agencies avoid duplicating examinations. Also, inasmuch as State member banks are subject to examination by State authorities, the Reserve Banks and these authorities cooperate, whenever feasible, in joint or alternate examinations. The established policy is for a Reserve Bank to conduct one regular examination of each State member bank every calendar year and to furnish a copy of the report and any related correspondence to the Board of Governors. Each Federal Reserve Bank obtains from the Comptroller's Regional Chief Examiners copies of reports of examination of national banks and exchanges reports with the Board of Governors, the Comptroller of the Currency, and the Federal Deposit Insurance Corporation in Washington.

Bank Supervision and Monetary Policy

It is sometimes suggested that bank supervisory standards be adjusted flexibly to help in counteracting cyclical instabilities in the economy. This suggestion would call for a firming of examination and other supervisory standards in periods of inflationary or speculative boom and a relaxation in periods of recession.

In considering this suggestion, one should bear in mind

that bank supervision involves recurrent, and not continuous, inspection of individual banks and by its nature entails a complex set of procedures evolved over many years. Such a process scarcely accommodates itself to a raising or a lowering of examination standards in response to changing economic conditions.

At the same time bank supervisory authorities are fully aware that banking difficulties have at times in the past intensified economic instability and that such risks should be reduced. Accordingly, modern supervisory appraisal of bank assets emphasizes sustainable banking values rather than current market values. In this way, bank supervisory authorities and examiners try to exclude from bank-asset valuation the transitory influences associated with economic fluctuations. All of the governmental agencies concerned now use this approach to bank supervision and examination.

While the general instruments of reserve banking are the appropriate means for influencing economic stability through credit and monetary policy, bank supervision contributes to an intimate, current understanding of banking conditions. In this respect, various questions that supervisory agencies ask in their examination of banks and their frequent communications with banks throughout the year supply information on bankers' activities and expectations that throw light on the developing bank credit situation. In effect, examination reports provide a continuous sampling of banking data. Some of the information derived from them—such as that suggestive of tendencies in the quality of bank credit advanced—would not easily be obtained otherwise. Such information is a valuable by-product of the bank supervision process.

Fundamentally, supervision contributes to the maintenance of economic stability through its effects on the internal strength of banks. To the extent that bank supervision fosters competition and helps individual banks under competent management to remain strong, it makes for an effective and responsive system of banks and enables banks to weather adverse conditions and serve their communities constructively in bad times as well as good.

CHAPTER XVII

SERVICE FUNCTIONS. *The Federal Reserve Banks handle the legal reserve accounts of member banks, furnish currency for circulation, facilitate the collection and clearance of checks, and act as fiscal agents of the U.S. Government.*

THE Federal Reserve System, in addition to being responsible for regulating the flow of credit and money and for bank supervision, performs a variety of regular services for member banks, the U.S. Government, and the public. This chapter describes the principal service functions of the Federal Reserve Banks.

The volume of service operations performed by the Reserve Banks for the banking system and the Treasury runs into huge figures, as the table on the next page shows. In 1962 these Banks transferred three trillion dollars of funds and handled more than one trillion dollars in checks. Both the composition and the volume of service operations vary considerably with short-term fluctuations in the levels of production, trade, and prices. Over the half century of the Federal Reserve System's existence, these operations

267

have grown rapidly as the financial resources of the nation have expanded.

VOLUME OF SELECTED FEDERAL RESERVE BANK OPERATIONS
1962

Type of operation	Number of pieces handled (thousands)[1]	Amounts handled (thousands of dollars)
Discounts and advances............	7	19,685,050
Currency received and counted:		
Paper currency.................	4,734,419	31,621,061
Coin..........................	10,213,309	1,140,009
Checks handled:		
Postal money orders............	247,400	4,701,516
U.S. Government checks........	443,271	125,431,359
All other[2].....................	3,873,341	1,283,430,670
Transfers of funds................	3,318	3,168,359,313
Issues, redemptions, and exchanges of U.S. Government securities....	198,123	639,755,488

[1] Packaged items handled as a single item are counted as one piece.
[2] Exclusive of checks drawn on the Federal Reserve Banks.

Handling Member Bank Reserve Accounts

A substantial part of the daily work of the Reserve Banks relates to member bank reserve accounts. Member banks use their reserve accounts much as individuals use their checking accounts in day-to-day transactions, drawing on them for making payments and replenishing them with funds that are received. For example, entries are made in these accounts as member banks obtain currency (paper money and coin) to pay out to their customers or as they redeposit currency in excess of the amount needed for circulation, and as checks are collected and cleared. Other entries arise as Treasury deposits are transferred from member banks to the Federal Reserve Banks, or as funds (member bank reserve deposits) are transferred by telegraph from one Reserve Bank to another for various purposes, or as a bank borrows from, or makes repayment to, a Reserve Bank. Various types of transactions are described in subsequent paragraphs. The Reserve Banks must record all transactions and strike a daily balance for the reserve account of each member bank.

Distributing Currency

There are two principal ways by which any individual gets paper money and coin. He may draw it out of his bank and have it charged to his account, or he may receive it as payment for his services or his merchandise. In the latter event, the currency received has usually been drawn out of a bank by someone else.

There are times when banks are called on to pay out more currency than they receive, and there are times when they receive more than they pay out. Moreover, the demand varies for different kinds of currency. Some communities use more coin and less paper money than others; and some use more of certain denominations.

The ready availability of currency at Federal Reserve Banks enables member banks to provide the amounts and kinds of currency that people in their communities want. When member banks need to replenish their currency supply, they order currency from their Reserve Bank and have it charged to their reserve accounts. Nonmember banks generally get their supplies from member banks.

To meet the varying demands for currency, the Reserve

269

Banks keep a large stock of paper money and coin on hand. This includes both Federal Reserve notes, which are Reserve Bank liabilities, and Treasury currency — silver certificates, United States notes, and coin. A Reserve Bank pays for Treasury currency by crediting the Treasury's deposit account for the amount obtained.

Collecting, Clearing, and Transferring Funds

Currency is indispensable, yet it is used mainly for the smaller transactions of present-day economic life. A century ago it was used far more generally. Since then the use of bank deposits has increased to such an extent that payments made by check are now many times larger than those made with paper money and coin. The use of checking deposits by business and the general public is facilitated by the service of the Federal Reserve Banks in clearing and collecting checks and in providing the mechanism through which commercial banks settle for the checks they clear and collect.

For example, suppose that a manufacturer in Hartford, Connecticut, sells $1,000 worth of electrical equipment to a dealer in Sacramento, California, and receives in payment a check that is drawn on a bank in Sacramento. The Hartford manufacturer deposits the check in a bank in Hartford.

The Hartford bank sends the check (together with other checks) to the Federal Reserve Bank of Boston for credit in its reserve account. The Boston Reserve Bank sends the check to the Federal Reserve Bank of San Francisco, which in turn sends it to the Sacramento bank. The Sacramento bank charges the check to the account of the depositor who wrote it and has the amount charged to its own reserve account at the San Francisco Reserve Bank. The Federal Reserve Bank of San Francisco remits the amount to the Federal Reserve Bank of Boston through the Interdistrict Settlement Fund.

Because promptness in collecting checks is important, the Federal Reserve Banks extend to member banks having a substantial volume of checks payable in other Federal Reserve districts the privilege of sending such checks directly to other Federal Reserve Banks for collection. The Hartford bank, therefore, might have forwarded the $1,000 check directly to the Federal Reserve Bank of San Francisco for collection, at the same time informing the Federal Reserve Bank of Boston of its action. On the basis of this information the Federal Reserve Bank of Boston would then have credited the Hartford bank's reserve account just as if the check had been sent through the Boston Bank.

The volume of checks handled by the Federal Reserve Banks has grown rapidly over the years, as the following chart shows. Many other checks are collected by large city banks for their correspondents and are not handled by the Reserve Banks. Banks collect checks payable locally through clearing houses or by presenting the checks directly to the banks on which they are drawn. The settlement or payment for most checks drawn on member banks, however, is made, directly or indirectly, through their reserve balances with the Federal Reserve Banks. Thus, the facilities of the Reserve Banks aid in clearing and collecting checks, whether they originate locally or across the country.

All checks collected and cleared through the Federal Reserve Banks must be paid in full by the banks on which they are drawn, without deduction of a fee or charge. That is, they must be payable at par; otherwise the Reserve Banks will not receive them for collection. Banks on the par list comprise all member banks and those nonmember banks that have agreed to remit at par for checks forwarded to them by the Federal Reserve Banks for payment. As of the end of 1962, about 93 per cent of all

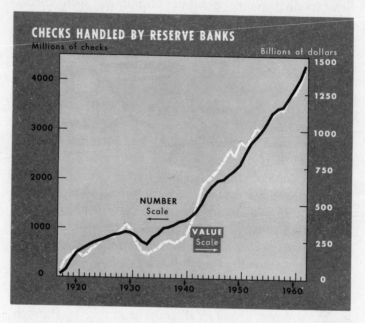

commercial banks and branches, accounting for about 98 per cent of all commercial bank deposits, were on the Federal Reserve par list.

Over the years the process of clearing and collecting checks has been greatly shortened and simplified. Both commercial banks and the Federal Reserve Banks have participated in this development. By doing so, they have improved the means of paying for goods and services and of settling monetary obligations; they have also reduced the cost to the public of making payments and transferring funds. Ways to achieve further improvements are under continuous consideration. For example, much of the manual burden of processing checks has been relieved by conversion of this work to electronic equipment.

In addition to checks, the Federal Reserve Banks handle other items for collection. These include such items as drafts, promissory notes, and bond coupons.

In order to make transfers and payments as promptly and efficiently as possible, the twelve Federal Reserve Banks maintain a gold certificate fund in Washington called the Interdistrict Settlement Fund. Each Reserve Bank has a share in it. This fund represents a substantial part of the gold certificate reserves of the Federal Reserve Banks. Through it money is constantly being transferred by telegraphic order from the account of one Reserve Bank to that of another.

On an average business day more than $7 billion of transfers and payments are made through the Interdistrict Settlement Fund. These are for the most part settlements for checks collected, transfers of balances for account of member banks and their customers, and transfers for the U.S. Treasury.

The cost of clearing and collecting checks and of supplying currency and coin is a major part of Federal Reserve Bank expenses. The Reserve Banks provide these services for member banks free of charge. This practice is consistent with the ideal of a money that circulates at par in all regions of the country.

273

Fiscal Agency Functions

The twelve Federal Reserve Banks carry the principal checking accounts of the U.S. Treasury, handle much of the work entailed in issuing and redeeming Government obligations, and perform numerous other important fiscal duties for the U.S. Government.

The Government is continuously receiving and spending funds in all parts of the United States. Its receipts come mainly from taxpayers and purchasers of Government securities and are deposited eventually in the Federal Reserve Banks to the credit of the Treasury. Its funds are disbursed mostly by check, and the checks are charged to Treasury accounts by the Reserve Banks.

When the Treasury offers a new issue of Government securities, the Reserve Banks receive the applications of banks, dealers, and others who wish to buy; make allotments of securities in accordance with instructions from the Treasury; deliver the securities to the purchasers; receive payment for them; and credit the amounts received to Treasury accounts. As brought out below, most of these payments are made initially to member and nonmember banks and are kept in Treasury tax and loan accounts at these banks.

Each Federal Reserve Bank administers for the Treasury the tax and loan deposit accounts of the banks in its district. Both member and nonmember banks, by complying with the Treasury's requirements, may become "special depositaries" of the Treasury and carry tax and loan deposit accounts. The principal requirement is the pledge with a Federal Reserve Bank, as fiscal agent of the Treasury, of enough Government securities or other acceptable collateral to secure fully the balance in the account.

For the convenience of the Treasury and also for the convenience of investors in Government securities, it is necessary to have facilities in various parts of the country to handle public debt transactions. The Federal Reserve Banks furnish these facilities. They redeem Government securities as they mature, make exchanges of denominations or kinds, pay interest coupons, and do a number of other things involved in servicing the Government debt. In addition they issue and redeem U.S. savings bonds and service the banks and other financial institutions designated as issuing and paying agents for such bonds.

Another part of the fiscal agency activities of the Federal Reserve Banks is their work in connection with the so-called "V-loan program." This program, authorized by the Defense Production Act of 1950 and implemented by Regulation V of the Board of Governors, is an arrangement to assist competent contractors and subcontractors who lack sufficient working capital to undertake defense contracts for the production of essential goods and materials. For this purpose the Departments of the Army, Navy, Air Force, Commerce, Interior, and Agriculture, the Defense Supply Agency of the Department of Defense, the General Services Administration, the National Aeronautics and Space Administration, and the Atomic Energy Commission are authorized to guarantee loans made by commercial banks and other private financing institutions. The Reserve Banks act as fiscal agents for the guaranteeing agencies in connection with such loans.

The Federal Reserve Banks may also perform fiscal agency services in connection with the financial activities of various Government lending agencies. They are reimbursed by the U.S. Treasury and other Government

275

agencies for much of the expense incurred in the performance of fiscal agency functions other than depositary functions.

Because of its location in one of the principal financial centers of the world, the Federal Reserve Bank of New York acts as the agent of the U.S. Treasury in gold and foreign exchange transactions. It acts as depositary for the International Monetary Fund, the International Bank for Reconstruction and Development, and other international organizations. It also receives deposits of foreign monetary authorities and performs certain incidental services as their correspondent. These services include handling short-term investments and holding earmarked gold.

All the Federal Reserve Banks participate in foreign accounts carried on the books of the Federal Reserve Bank of New York. In these matters the New York Reserve Bank acts as agent for the other Federal Reserve Banks. The Board of Governors in Washington exercises special supervision over all relationships and transactions of Federal Reserve Banks with foreign monetary authorities and with international organizations.

Preparedness for National Defense

The Board of Governors is responsible for the development of national security preparedness measures relating to bank credit and monetary policies. In cooperation with the Department of the Treasury (including the Comptroller of the Currency), the Federal Deposit Insurance Corporation, and others, it is also responsible for preparedness programs relating to the operation of the banking system. The Federal Reserve Banks are responsible for providing commercial banks with instructions on the distribution of currency, the collection of checks, and the availability of credit for essential purposes in an emergency. These preparedness responsibilities of the Board of Governors and the Federal Reserve Banks are a part of the over-all defense program of the Government to assure the nation's readiness to meet economic and financial needs related to any wartime emergency.

———————

SELECTED FEDERAL RESERVE PUBLICATIONS

(List appears on following pages)

BOARD OF GOVERNORS

ANNUAL REPORT. (No charge.)

FEDERAL RESERVE BULLETIN. Monthly. (Subscription price, $6.00 a year or 60 cents a copy; foreign mailing, $7.00 a year or 70 cents a copy. Group subscriptions in the United States for 10 or more copies to one address, 50 cents per copy per month, or $5.00 for 12 months. Reprints of selected articles are available free of charge upon request.)

FEDERAL RESERVE CHART BOOK: FINANCIAL AND BUSINESS STATISTICS. Monthly. Annual subscription includes one issue of Historical Chart Book. (Subscription price, $6.00 a year or 60 cents a copy; in quantities of 10 or more copies of the same issue for single shipment, 50 cents each; foreign mailing, $7.00 a year or 70 cents a copy.)

FEDERAL RESERVE HISTORICAL CHART BOOK. Issued annually in September. Subscription to monthly chart book includes one issue of the Historical. (60 cents a copy; in quantities of 10 or more for single shipment, 50 cents each; foreign mailing, 70 cents each.)

ALL-BANK STATISTICS, 1896-1955. April 1959. 1,229 pages ($4.00 a copy.)

FEDERAL FUNDS MARKET. A study by a Federal Reserve System Committee. May 1959. 111 pages. ($1.00 a copy; in quantities of 10 or more for single shipment, 85 cents each.)

THE FEDERAL RESERVE ACT, as amended through October 1, 1961, with an appendix containing provisions of certain other statutes affecting the Reserve System. 386 pages. ($1.25 a copy.)

FLOW OF FUNDS IN THE UNITED STATES, 1939-53. December 1955. 390 pages. ($2.75 a copy.)

INDUSTRIAL PRODUCTION—1957-59 Base. 1962. 172 pages. ($1.00 a copy; in quantities of 10 or more for single shipment, 85 cents each.)

MONETARY POLICY AND MANAGEMENT OF THE PUBLIC DEBT: A SELECTED BIBLIOGRAPHY. This list (mimeographed) is revised or supplemented annually. (No charge.)

PUBLICATIONS

TREASURY-FEDERAL RESERVE STUDY OF THE GOVERNMENT SECURITIES MARKET. Part I. 1959. 108 pages. Part II. 1960. 159 pages. Part III. 1960. 112 pages. (Individual books, $1.00 each; set of 3 books, $2.50.)

Copies of this book, THE FEDERAL RESERVE SYSTEM: PURPOSES AND FUNCTIONS, may be obtained without charge, either individually or in quantities for classroom and other use.

In addition to the publications listed, the Board issues periodic releases, other special studies, and reprints. Lists of available material may be obtained upon request. Inquiries regarding publications should be directed to the Division of Administrative Services, Board of Governors of the Federal Reserve System, Washington, D.C. 20551.

Federal Reserve Banks

BOSTON

Time Deposits in New England. A survey of the historical development of time and savings deposits, with special emphasis on conditions in New England. (Federal Reserve Bank of Boston, 1962 Annual Report, pages 3-61.) (No charge.)

CHICAGO

Modern Money Mechanics: A Workbook on Deposits, Currency, and Bank Reserves. Text and "T account" description of the money-creation process and the factors affecting member bank reserves. 1961. 32 pages. (No charge.)

The Two Faces of Debt. A description of the economic role of debt and the amounts owed by various sectors. 1963. 20 pages. (No charge.)

CLEVELAND

Money Market Instruments. 1962. 32 pages. (No charge.)

KANSAS CITY

Essays on Commercial Banking, by D. A. Cawthorne, Sam B. Chase, Jr., and Lyle E. Gramley. Nine essays on various aspects of commercial bank policies and operations. August 1962. 98 pages. (No charge.)

A Study of Scale Economies in Banking, by Lyle E. Gramley. A study of costs and earnings of commercial banks as related to their size. November 1962. 60 pages. (No charge.)

MINNEAPOLIS

Your Money and the Federal Reserve System (rev. ed.). An illustrated elementary discussion of the work of the Federal Reserve System. 1957. 20 pages. (No charge.)

PUBLICATIONS

NEW YORK

DEPOSIT VELOCITY AND ITS SIGNIFICANCE, by George Garvy. November 1959. 88 pages. (60 cents a copy; 30 cents a copy on orders from educational institutions.)

FEDERAL RESERVE OPERATIONS IN THE MONEY AND GOVERNMENT SECURITIES MARKET, by Robert V. Roosa. July 1956. 105 pages. (No charge.)

MONEY: MASTER OR SERVANT? An explanation in nontechnical language of the role of money in our economy. 2nd edition, April 1960. 48 pages. (No charge.)

THE MONEY SIDE OF "THE STREET," by Carl H. Madden. An account of the workings of the New York money market. September 1959. 104 pages. (70 cents a copy; 35 cents a copy on orders from educational institutions.)

OPEN MARKET OPERATIONS. An explanation in nontechnical terms of the translation of broad monetary objectives into day-to-day operations. January 1963. 43 pages. (No charge.)

PHILADELPHIA

DEFENDING THE DOLLAR, by Clay J. Anderson. A discussion of the balance of payments, the foreign exchange market, and the defense of the dollar against outflows of funds. November 1962. 27 pages. (No charge.)

HOW TO INTERPRET FEDERAL RESERVE REPORTS. January 1962. 48 pages. (No charge.)

MONETARY POLICY—DECISION-MAKING, TOOLS, AND OBJECTIVES. This collection of articles deals with some of the problems encountered in implementing monetary policy. April 1961. 52 pages. (No charge.)

THE QUEST FOR STABILITY. Five essays describing efforts to achieve an efficient monetary system in the United States. 1954. 54 pages. (No charge.)

284

RICHMOND

THE FEDERAL RESERVE AT WORK, by B. U. Ratchford and Robert P. Black. A discussion in layman's terms of the structure, objectives, and functions of the Federal Reserve System. 2nd edition, 1962. 30 pages. (No charge.)

FEDERAL RESERVE BANK DIRECTORS, by Welford S. Farmer. A description of the role of the head office and branch directors in the operation of the Federal Reserve Banks and their contribution to the functioning of the economy. 19 pages. (No charge.)

NOTES ON CENTRAL BANKS, by B. U. Ratchford and Jimmie R. Monhollon. A booklet dealing with the nature, characteristics, and functions of central banks, with special reference to the Federal Reserve System. March 1963. 33 pages. (No charge.)

READINGS ON MONEY. A discussion of the nature of money and the processes of its creation and circulation. 3rd edition, 1963. 58 pages. (No charge.)

Each Federal Reserve Bank also publishes a monthly review of credit and business conditions which will be sent regularly to anyone requesting it. Some of the Banks issue booklets on special subjects, such as agricultural credit and economic indicators.

Requests for the reviews and other Bank publications, and inquiries about quantity orders, should be sent to the Federal Reserve Banks at the following addresses:

Federal Reserve Bank of Atlanta
Atlanta, Georgia 30303

Federal Reserve Bank of Boston
Boston, Massachusetts 02106

Federal Reserve Bank of Chicago
Chicago, Illinois 60690

Federal Reserve Bank of Cleveland
Cleveland, Ohio 44101

PUBLICATIONS

Federal Reserve Bank of Dallas
Dallas, Texas 75222

Federal Reserve Bank of Kansas City
Kansas City, Missouri 64106

Federal Reserve Bank of Minneapolis
Minneapolis, Minnesota 55440

Federal Reserve Bank of New York
New York, New York 10045

Federal Reserve Bank of Philadelphia
Philadelphia, Pennsylvania 19101

Federal Reserve Bank of Richmond
Richmond, Virginia 23213

Federal Reserve Bank of St. Louis
St. Louis, Missouri 63166

Federal Reserve Bank of San Francisco
San Francisco, California 94120

INDEX

Acceptances, bankers'....................................31, 110, 190
Annual Reports, Board of Governors........................244, 245

Balance of international payments:
  Accounts..150-53
  Chart... 153
  Definition..150-52
  Factors influencing.......................................156-58
  Federal Reserve policy and................................149-63
  Foreign currency operations (*See* Federal
    Open Market Committee)
  Gold conversions and...................................... 155
  Monetary policy and.......................................158-60
  Open Market Committee operations and.....................33, 36
  Problem of..210-12
  Relationship to domestic economic activity.................. 12
  Significance... 155
  Swap arrangements.....................................162, 192
Balance sheet of the Federal Reserve Banks....................187-89
Bank:
  Credit..4, 10, 30, 76-78, 165, 265
  Examinations..4, 21, 259-66
  Examiners... 260
  Reserve equations...............................199-213, 217, 219
  Reserve factors.................................199-213, 215
  Reserves (*See* Reserves)
  Supervision:
    Federal Reserve functions...............................257-66
    Government agencies and................................. 261
    Monetary policy and....................................264-66
    Scope..258, 262-64
Bank for International Settlements............................ 162
Bank Holding Company Act.................................... 263
Bankers' acceptances.....................................31, 110, 190
Banking Act of *1935*... 50
Banking system, operation of reserves in......................66-69
Board of Governors.......................20-23, 225-28, 247, 276
Businesses:
  Demands for credit..102-04
  Nonfinancial, in credit markets........................... 102
  Sources of credit..96-98

287

INDEX

Capital accounts.. 195
Capital assets, costs of producing new assets................... 140
Capital markets.. 86
Cash:
    Demands for.. 133
    Monetary policy and...................................... 135
Central banks...4, 194
Central reserve cities.. 3
Charts:
    Bank Reserve Equation.................................... 203
    Change in Financial Position............................... 93
    Checks Handled by Reserve Banks........................... 272
    Coupon Rate, Market Yield, and Price....................... 109
    Credit Expansion.. 84
    Currency and Federal Reserve Credit........................ 183
    Currency in Circulation.................................... 181
    Deposits and Bank Lending................................. 76
    Discount and Bill Rates.................................... 48
    Disposition of Federal Reserve Bank Earnings................ 196
    Federal Reserve Credit.................................... 59
    Flow of Federal Reserve Influence.......................... 129
    Government Security Transactions, *1962*.................... 36
    Gross National Product and Money Supply................... 146
    Gross National Saving..................................... 94
    Kinds of Currency.. 179
    Long- and Short-Term Interest Rates....................... 111
    Member Bank Reserves.................................... 79
    Money and Near-Moneys................................... 7
    Organization of the Federal Reserve System................. 22
    Process of Deposit Expansion.............................. 72
    Production and Prices..................................... 209
    Rates on Bank Loans to Business........................... 86
    Relation of Parts of the Federal Reserve System
        to Instruments of Credit Policy......................... 227
    Relationships Among Reserve Measures...................... 250
    Reserves and Borrowings.................................. 222
    Reserves of Federal Reserve Banks......................... 173
    Selected Interest Rates.................................... 113
    Total U.S. Gold Stock..................................... 168
    U.S. Balance of Payments.................................. 153

Charts—Continued
U.S. Government Marketable Debt............................ 89
Yields and Prices on U.S. Government Securities.............. 115
Check clearing and collection...............................194, 270-73
Commercial banks............2, 25, 40, 63, 70, 84, 89, 99, 100, 272, 276
Comptroller of the Currency...........................26, 262, 264
Condition statements of the Reserve Banks, weekly.........187, 215, 216
Conferences of Chairmen of the Reserve Banks................. 24
Conferences of Presidents of the Reserve Banks.................. 24
Contract interest rates....................................... 108
Coupon rates...108-10
Credit:
    Bank..............................4, 10, 30, 76-78, 165, 265
    Demands for...101-04
    Expansion (chart).. 84
    Federal Reserve..................................59, 165, 201, 204
    Funds, supply and demand...............................94-104
    Markets:
        Competition for funds...............................104-06
        Definition... 83
        Geographical distribution.............................86-88
        Interest rates... 107
        Nature of..85-88
        Net reserve positions and.............................. 222
        Role of economic groups...............................92-94
        U.S. Government securities (*See* Government
            securities market)
    Mortgages.. 142
    Policy:
        Effect on borrowers.................................138-43
        Federal Reserve...................................197, 206-10
        Relation of parts to instruments of (chart).................. 227
    Regulation of... 9
    Short- and intermediate-term.............................. 141
    Sources..94-101
    Stock market, regulation of.....................55-57, 61, 228
Credit and money:
    Bank...4, 5, 10, 30
    Effect of changes in.....................................10-13
    Forces affecting flow of.................................. 9
    Regulation of... 4, 59

Currency:
  Before *1914*.. 177
  Circulation.........................180-82, 201, 204, 206, 208, 210
  Demands for..180-82, 269
  Distribution of.. 269
  Dollars as an international reserve......................... 155
  Elasticity of..1, 177
  Federal Reserve credit and (chart)......................... 183
  Federal Reserve notes.....................166, 178-80, 188, 192
  Kinds (chart)... 179
  Relation to reserve banking...............................177-85
  Treasury...177, 180

Deposits:
  Bank lending and.....................................73, 74-76
  Demand, as money... 6
  Demand, ratios of reserves to............................66-69
  Expansion (chart).. 72
  Foreign central banks...................................... 194
  Liabilities...192-95
  Savings and other time................................70, 228
  Treasury accounts.. 193
  Treasury tax and loan accounts........................194, 274
  U.S. banks, *June 30, 1963*................................ 25
Directors:
  Federal Reserve Banks...................................... 19
  Member banks..262-63
Discount:
  Administration.......................................42, 230-32
  Bill rates and (chart)..................................... 48
  Operations..29, 40-50, 230
  Rates..............40, 45-49, 59, 124, 210, 212, 228, 230-32, 239-40
Discounting..40, 57
Discounts:
  Effect on reserves... 41
  Member banks..................................43-45, 58, 190

Earnings, Reserve Bank..................................... 196
Economic stability... 127
Examinations, bank.............................4, 21, 259-66
Exchange Stabilization Fund..........................161, 168

Federal Advisory Council.................................... 23
Federal Deposit Insurance Corporation.....................262, 264
Federal funds market.......................................49, 255
Federal Open Market Account............................31, 39, 233
Federal Open Market Account Manager
   and Special Manager...............31, 233, 239, 241, 244-49, 252-56
Federal Open Market Committee
   (*See also* Open market operations):
   Directives...246-56
   Foreign currency operations................29, 39, 160-63, 242, 245
   Function.. 23
   Meetings:
      Agenda.. 242
      Frequency... 232
      Organization of..241-44
      Preparation for... 240
   Monetary policy role.. 238
   Operation of.. 31
   Organization.. 232
   Policy:
      Directives......................................239, 244, 246-56
      Execution..245-56
      Procedures.......................................33, 239-44
Federal Reserve Act.................................1, 4, 17, 24, 26
Federal Reserve Agents............................19, 178, 179-80
Federal Reserve Banks:
   Balance sheets of..187-89
   Branches.. 17
   Capital stock..26, 195
   Credit policy... 197
   Directors... 19
   Districts... 17
   Earnings.. 196
   Examinations...21, 264
   Fiscal agency functions....................................274-76
   Foreign accounts..194, 276
   Gold certificate accounts...........................167, 169, 170
   New York Bank..........161, 170, 171, 230, 232, 233, 247, 255, 276
   Obligations and privileges.................................. 26
   Officers.. 20
   Representation at Federal Open Market
      Committee meetings................................240, 242-43

Federal Reserve Banks—Continued
    Role in decision-making...................................230-33
    Service functions...267-77
    Surpluses... 196
    Volume of service operations.............................. 267
Federal Reserve Bulletins...................................... 213
Federal Reserve notes.................166, 178-80, 184, 188, 192, 270
Federal Reserve System:
    Authority, distribution of................................. 226
    Decentralization.. 18
    Establishment... 1
    Functions..........................1, 4, 257, 262-64, 267, 268-77
    Influence, flow of (chart)................................. 129
    Influence on credit and money............................. 8-10
    Map... 16
    Membership.. 24
    Monetary policy, organization for.........................225-34
    Open market policy process................................235-56
    Organization chart.. 22
    Policy-making:
        Complexities..236-38
        Federal Open Market Committee role.................... 238
        Guides in... 237
    Publications, selected.................................... 279
    Relation of parts to instruments of credit policy (chart)......... 227
    Relations with other Government agencies................37, 228-30
    Structure...15-24
    Treasury accord with...................................... 207
"Feel of the market"... 251
Financial institutions, in credit markets......................99, 103
Financial position changes (chart)............................ 93
Fiscal agency functions.......................................274-76
Float...192, 195, 220
Foreign banks.......................................194, 220, 263
Foreign currency operations
    (*See* Federal Open Market Committee)

Gold:
    Balance of international payments (*See* Balance of
        international payments)
    Bank reserve factors and.................................. 201
    Certificate accounts................................167, 169, 170

Gold—Continued
Certificate reserves...................166, 173-75, 178, 188, 197, 273
Certificates, Treasury issued.............................. 188
"Earmarked".. 171
International transactions................................. 168
Monetization of..169-72
Movements.......................................171, 172, 206
Price.. 167
Reserve banking and......................................165-75
Reserve money..166-69
Reserves, basis of Federal Reserve credit..................... 165
Stock, total U.S. (chart).................................. 168
Title to...167, 171
Treasury holdings... 167
Gold Reserve Act of 1934................................. 166
Government marketable debt (chart).......................... 89
Government securities:
Definition.. 191
Federal Reserve Banks' processing of........................ 274
Market:
Activity... 90
Federal Reserve support of............................. 207
Open market operations and....................34, 37, 233, 255
Services... 91
Size... 88
Transactions, 1962 (chart).............................. 36
Yields and prices.. 115
Governments, in credit markets.........................98, 102, 103
Gross National Product and Money Supply (chart).............. 146
Gross National Saving (chart)............................... 94

Interdistrict Settlement Fund............................271, 273
Interest, definition....................................... 118
Interest rates:
Bank loans to business (chart)............................ 86
Changes.......................................116, 136-38, 139
Contract.. 108
Definition... 107
Differences...110-12
Expectations and... 119
Federal Reserve actions and..........................30, 123-25
Fluctuations.. 110

INDEX

Interest rates—Continued
Inflexibilities.. 122
Long- and short-term...........................111, 114-17, 159
Monetary policy and....................................123-25
Money and bank credit and............................. 121
Movements..112-16
Selected (chart).. 113
International Bank for Reconstruction and Development......... 276
International Monetary Fund.............................. 276
International payments:
Dollars..154, 168
Gold...154, 168
International reserves, dollar holdings as...................... 155

Lending agencies, Federal................................ 275
Loans and investments...............................66-69, 74-76

Margin requirements...................................55-57, 61
Member banks:
Borrowing...43-45, 57, 58
Classes... 24
Deposits.. 25
Examinations..262, 264
Number.. 24
Obligations and privileges................................ 26
Officers and directors.................................... 263
Reserve requirements (*See* Reserve requirements)
Reserves (*See* Reserves)
Supervision 262-64
Monetary instruments, coordination.......................57-62
Monetary policy:
Aims.. 127
Balance of international payments and....................158-60
Bank supervision and..................................264-66
Economic growth and..................................145-47
Effects on:
Borrowing and spending................................ 138
Commercial banks....................................130-32
Lenders and savers..................................... 137
Nonbank lenders....................................... 137
Spending.. 143
"Even keel"... 38

Monetary policy—Continued
    Influences... 128
    Interest rates and...................................107, 123-25
    Net reserve positions and...........................222, 248-51
    Open market policy process..............................235-56
    Organization of Federal Reserve System for.................225-34
    Treasury coordination....................................... 229
Monetary regulation, instruments............................ 29
Money (*See also* Credit and money):
    Creation of... 75
    Definition.. 5
    Gold as reserve money...................................166-69
    "High-powered"..69, 77
    Markets.. 86
    Near-moneys and... 7, 8
    Supply, effect of changes in............................... 132
Mutual savings banks:
    Number and deposits....................................... 25
    Sources of credit funds.................................... 101

National Advisory Council on International Monetary
    and Financial Problems.................................... 230
National Bank Act... 26
National banks:
    Charters... 26
    Examinations.. 264
    Number and deposits.....................................24-25
    Reserves... 3
    System membership... 24
National defense.. 276
National Monetary Commission.............................. 4
Near-moneys.. 7, 8
Net reserve positions...................................223, 248-51
Nonbank lenders... 137
Nonmember banks.......................................25, 194

Open Market Account...............................31, 39, 233
Open Market Committee (*See* Federal
    Open Market Committee)
Open market operations..............29-39, 57, 58-60, 61, 208-10, 238

Par lists... 272
Production and prices (chart)............................... 209

Regulations, Board of Governors:
  A (discount process)......................................42, 231
  V (defense production loans)............................... 275
Repurchase agreements......................................31, 191
Reserve:
  Balances.. 80
  Banking (*See also* Monetary policy)......................... 127
  Banks, foreign.. 4
  Measures, relationships among (chart)....................... 250
  Money, multiplying capacity................................. 73
  Ratios...66-68, 197, 239
Reserve requirements:
  Changes in.....................29, 50-55, 57, 174, 212, 226, 239-40
  Federal Reserve Banks............................178-80, 182-84
  Member banks...................................51, 65, 70, 80
  Suspension of... 174
Reserves:
  Borrowings and (chart)...................................... 222
  Changes, short-term..215-24
  Currency circulation and...................................182-85
  Federal Reserve Bank (chart)............................... 173
  Free..223, 224, 249
  Function of...64-81
  Gold certificate.........................173-75, 178, 188, 197, 273
  Member banks:
    Balances................................80, 248-51, 267, 268
    Bank reserve equations................................199-213
    Changes....................................29, 204, 235
    Chart.. 79
    Excesses... 80
    Gold purchases or sales, effect............................ 172
    Measure of...248, 255
    Ratios..66-68
    Supplies... 248
    Treasury payments, effect.................................. 220
  Multiplying power..71-74
  Open market operations and............................247, 255
  Operation in banking system................................ 66
  Wartime and postwar.......................................205-07

Saving, gross national (chart)................................. 94
Saving-investment process....................................117-19

Savings and loan associations...............................89, 101
Savings institutions, in credit markets.........................95, 98
Securities, purchases or sales of............................3, 31, 35
Service functions, Federal Reserve Banks......................267-77
State member banks:
    Examinations..4, 264
    Number and deposits.................................... 25
    Obligations and privileges.................................. 26
Stock market credit, regulation........................55-57, 61, 228
Supervisory functions, Federal Reserve.................4, 257, 262-64
Surplus.. 196
Swap agreements... 162

Tax and loan accounts....................................193, 274
Transfer of funds...270-73
Treasury, U.S.:
    Currency.. 180
    Federal Reserve accord.................................33, 207
    Fiscal agency services for...............................274-76
    Gold certificate accounts................................. 167
    Gold holdings... 167
    Notes 177
    Payments... 219
    Relation of Federal Reserve with.......................37, 228-30
    Tax and loan deposit accounts..........................193, 274

United States notes..................................167, 180, 270

V-loan program... 275

Weekly condition statements of the Federal Reserve Banks........ 187